MIDWESTERN MILLIONAIRE

HARDWORKING · FRUGAL · DILIGENT SAVER

Enjoy the free book...
MWM's love free! :)

MIDWESTERN MILLIONAIRE
Hardworking · Frugal · Diligent Saver

Copyright © 2025 Joe F. Schmitz Jr.
All rights reserved.

ISBN: 978-1-964046-54-9

Expert Press
www.ExpertPress.net

The information provided in this book is for informational purposes only and is not intended to be a source of advice or credit analysis with respect to the material presented. The information and/or documents contained in this book do not constitute legal or financial advice and should never be used without first consulting with an insurance and/or a financial professional to determine what may be best for your individual needs.

The publisher and the author do not make any guarantee or other promise as to any results that may be obtained from using the content of this book. You should never make any investment decision without first consulting with your own financial advisor and conducting your own research and due diligence. To the maximum extent permitted by law, the publisher and the author disclaim any and all liability in the event any information, commentary, analysis, opinions, advice, and/or recommendations contained in this book prove to be inaccurate, incomplete, or unreliable or result in any investment or other losses.

Although the author and publisher have made every effort to ensure that the information in this book was correct at press time, the author and publisher do not assume and hereby disclaim any liability to any party for any loss, damage, or disruption caused by errors or omissions, whether such errors or omissions result from negligence, accident, or any other cause.

Content contained or made available through this book is not intended to and does not constitute legal advice or investment advice, and no attorney-client relationship is formed. The publisher and the author are providing this book and its contents on an "as is" basis. Your use of the information in this book is at your own risk.

MIDWESTERN MILLIONAIRE

HARDWORKING • FRUGAL • DILIGENT SAVER

JOE F. SCHMITZ JR.,
CFP®, CHFC®, CKA®

This book means a lot to me...

It was written to speak to people like my Uncle Chuck.

A man who worked twelve-hour days, raised five kids, and never made millions of dollars a year. But because of his diligence, he did the right things financially to retire comfortably. Unfortunately, my uncle passed away on January 15, 2023. The last time I spoke to my uncle, he told me, "Always trust the young guy." He was grateful for my advanced help in an area where he was not an expert and did not know who to trust to help him. He didn't know the advanced tax strategies and investment management he needed for retirement. Uncle Chuck was my first client when I started in the financial planning industry and that meant the world to me. Without people like him, I wouldn't be where I am today.

This book was written as a tribute to Uncle Chuck and all the other "Midwestern Millionaires" who taught me how to work hard and do the right thing. Teaching me how to look people in the eye, shake their hand, and get the job done. Period.

This book is to help those in or near retirement to make the most of their hard-earned life savings.

CONTENTS

Introduction: Who Is This "Midwestern Millionaire"?		1
1	**The Traits of a Midwestern Millionaire**	7
	Frozen Blueberries	12
2	**Why We Serve the Midwestern Millionaire**	15
	Is a Midwestern Millionaire Wealthy?	19
3	**What Must a Midwestern Millionaire Do?**	21
	Ten Actions	22
	Protect and Maximize	28
4	**Taxes—Are You Overpaying?**	31
	Tax Planning	33
	Investment Planning	34
	Income Planning	34
	Healthcare Planning	35
	Estate Planning	35
	Legislative Risk: Is the Tax Code Written in Pencil?	36
5	**Which Buckets Hold Your Life Savings?**	41
	The Taxable Bucket	42
	The Tax-Deferred Bucket	44
	The Tax-Free Bucket	51
6	**Advanced Strategies for the Tax Buckets**	55
	The Tax Buckets in Summary	67
7	**Social Security Strategies**	69
	Social Security Tax Torpedo	70
8	**Medicare Premium Strategies**	81
	Uncle Sam and Aunt IRMAA	82
9	**Estate Planning and Transferring Wealth**	85
	Do You Need a Trust?	88
	What Are Estate Taxes?	92
	Additional Protection for You and Your Family: Personal Liability Umbrella Policy	98
	Spousal Planning and the Widow(er)'s Penalty	99
	The Kiddo's Penalty	101
	Gifting and Giving	102
	A Multidisciplinary Team: Consolidation and Collaboration	104
10	**The Purpose of Money**	107
	Peak Stamp of Approval	108
	Dream, Vision, Mission . . . and Purpose	109
11	**Why People Work with Us (or with a Holistic Team like Us)**	117
Sneak Peek of Joe's First Book, *I Hate Taxes*		125
About the Author		143

INTRODUCTION

WHO IS THIS "MIDWESTERN MILLIONAIRE"?

The "Midwestern Millionaire" is a term and concept that was inspired by our clients. It's a way to describe the crowd that my firm, Peak Retirement Planning, Inc., has worked with over the years. Who is a Midwestern Millionaire? Or rather—who are they?

Midwestern Millionaires are people who have gone to work every day and earned and saved consistently. In short, they have done what they were supposed to do for over thirty years to accumulate wealth. Doing everything they were told and doing it successfully:

- Saving at least 10–20 percent into their 401(k)

- Avoiding high-interest debt

- Buying a home

- Spending less than they make

A Midwestern Millionaire is someone who has saved at least $1 million and has traditional American Midwestern values such as hard work, frugality, and practicality. They also view themselves as responsible for stewarding this money well and not making mistakes managing it so they can enjoy the retirement they've worked hard for.

Because of their values and financial situation, these people are most worried about *protecting* the wealth they've worked hard to accumulate. This means they don't want to overpay in taxes. They will definitely pay their fair share but not a penny more. They understand the tax system is complex and ever-changing, and they know they need expert knowledge and proactive planning to get this piece of the puzzle in place.

They also want to ensure they have the right investment strategy in place to optimize their risk/return on their hard-earned life savings. We often tell the Midwestern Millionaire they can take as much risk as they want or as little risk as they want at this point in their life since they have enough saved to meet their goals. This often looks like having enough money protected to cover short-term needs while seeking growth on money geared for the future.

Protecting their wealth also means ensuring they know exactly how much income they must spend, and they will never overspend. They want to pay their own way to their last breath so as not to be a burden to others. We must tell this crowd to spend more money, as they are better savers than spenders (I discuss this further in chapter 10). They're experiencing a paradigm shift now that they have enough money and financial freedom.

Running out of money is the biggest fear for retirees, but for the Midwestern Millionaire, it doesn't have to be as big of a concern. Instead, they can do what they want when they want with whom they want—without that lingering fear. They just need a better plan to best steward their money toward their purpose.

The next piece of their planning is to think ahead about healthcare. They understand healthcare might be an expensive matter in the years to come and that Medicare's traditional plan isn't the be-all and end-all of healthcare coverage. They're also concerned about overpaying for Medicare because of the income-related monthly adjustment amount (IRMAA). They'll need to find supplemental coverage, or maybe prepare for an early retirement and decide what healthcare coverage will be best for them before Medicare kicks in at age sixty-five.

The last piece of the Midwestern Millionaire's planning is to consider estate planning. What happens at the end of their lives and after their death? First, they ensure their spouse is taken care of. Second, they want to leave behind a legacy of achievements, or they want to benefit their heirs through financial bequests. They definitely don't want Uncle Sam to take it all.

The Midwestern Millionaire is aware these five types of planning are needed and that they need expert assistance to perform that planning. We help our Midwestern Millionaire clients through our signature 5 Pillar Approach to retirement planning by addressing their tax, investment, income, healthcare, and estate planning. Putting all the pillars in place ensures that no stone is left unturned and we don't miss anything in their retirement plan.

The point of this book is to make you aware that the financial planning required for the Midwestern Millionaire's retirement years is more complex than the average American's. By reading this book, you will gain an understanding of the many concerns our clients have and the many strategies we use to maximize their hard-earned life savings. We do our best to squeeze out every drop of those savings to allow them to have more money to do what they want with their retirement. We often call this planning "owning your retirement."

My idea for this concept of the Midwestern Millionaire came from the book *The Millionaire Next Door: The Surprising Secrets of America's Wealthy* by Dr. Thomas J. Stanley and William D. Danko.[1] The authors reveal that the people with wealth aren't always the ones with the biggest houses and the nicest cars. The "wealthy" are those who have been frugal in their spending and diligent in their saving throughout their lives.

They didn't make incomes of $1 million a year; they're hardworking folks who may have never made more than $100,000–$200,000 per year most of their working lives. They put in thirty to forty or more years of daily hard work and diligently saved from every paycheck. They have saved into their retirement accounts, where it's common to see a net worth of at least $1 million. They have their house paid off, and their home has appreciated in value over the years due to maintenance and care, which adds to their net worth.

---

[1] Thomas J. Stanley and William D. Danko, *The Millionaire Next Door: The Surprising Secrets of America's Wealthy* (Taylor Trade Publishing, 2010).

They can also be known as the "Middle-Class Millionaires" because of these traits.

I'm from a rural community where this type of individual or family is common. We work with many Midwestern Millionaires. You better believe it's a term our clients love, and they proudly own it, saying, "Yes, that's me." Some have even said we should have a picture of them on the cover of this book.

1

THE TRAITS OF A MIDWESTERN MILLIONAIRE

Let me be clear about the Midwestern Millionaire. This isn't about American geography. You don't have to live in the Midwest to be a Midwestern Millionaire. We work with people living all across the country, and many of our clients who live on the East or West Coast and down South meet these criteria and have the same values as Midwesterners.

The following list outlines eight of the key traits we see in the Midwestern Millionaire:

1. Diligent Saver

As mentioned, the Midwestern Millionaire has saved at least $1 million. This is no easy accomplishment, considering all the things life can throw at you over the years. They have done this by being . . .

2. Frugal

Midwestern Millionaires are great savers and the worst spenders. That's how I like to explain it. It is that pair of "money habits" that has allowed them to accumulate their wealth.

They often like saving money on ordinary purchases, and they're content without having the most luxurious items. They're frugal; it's second nature to them. If they find blueberries on sale at the store, they stock up. At the end of this chapter, I'll tell a funny story about blueberries to emphasize this trait, which goes hand-in-hand with . . .

3. Hardworking

Midwestern Millionaires are willing to do whatever it takes, however long it takes. They are conscientious and consistent workers. They put their head down and get things done. My parents are two of the hardest workers I know and couldn't be better examples of Midwestern Millionaires.

My dad taught me that the day isn't over until the job is done. My mom taught me that you must give 100 percent in everything you do, often saying, "How you do anything is how you do everything."

They do everything needed because as Midwestern Millionaires, they . . .

4. Want to Pay Less in Taxes

They believe their hard-earned income and their life savings should be in their pockets and not in Uncle Sam's. They never want to overpay in taxes. Now, they're not against paying taxes, but they only want to pay their fair share and not "tip" Uncle Sam anything extra. They believe the government isn't necessarily the best steward of their taxpaying dollars. They believe in lowering taxes to allow for "We the People" to have more control over the economy, as opposed to giving more to the government and allowing them to control how our money is spent. People with Midwestern values also typically don't believe in handouts; they believe what you get is earned and not given.

The more money you have, the more tax you pay. Midwestern Millionaires know they will pay lots of taxes over their retirement unless they start successfully implementing tax-planning strategies now. They're also . . .

5. Risk-Averse

They want to protect their savings. Midwestern Millionaires are more conservative in their investing approach and want to find investments that are less aggressive and more stable and consistent over time. Yes, they want a return, but they don't want to take on more risk than they need to. They may want to achieve single and doubles now instead of swinging for the fences.

They also want to protect their wealth from healthcare bills (they've heard or seen how medical costs can be extremely costly throughout retirement). They strive to ensure that their wealth will transfer to their spouse and children without losing any of that wealth. They don't want to miss anything. This proves they are also . . .

6. Family-Oriented

Family is extremely important to Midwestern Millionaires. I've always been told to take care of those who take care of me. Likewise, many of our clients truly care about making sure their family is taken care of.

Our clients want their spouse to be taken care of when they pass away, and they want their kids and grandkids to have the opportunities and resources that will set them up for success. We can help them build financial plans that prepare for the loss of a spouse and build generational wealth for their families in the future.

One way we do this is through advanced tax planning. Midwestern Millionaires love learning about and implementing strategies that will ensure their family gets more of their wealth than Uncle Sam. We also do smart estate planning using strategies that allow the smooth transfer of assets to the next generation. We see that as not only having estate documents (which are extremely important) but also by having a rock-solid estate plan that incorporates advanced tax planning and purpose.

Midwestern Millionaires know they are blessed with wealth, but they remain . . .

7. Humble

You would never know the Midwestern Millionaire is a millionaire and has had extreme success over their lifetime. They don't always drive a flashy car or live in the biggest house. They don't participate in the latest fashion trends or spend thousands of dollars on clothing. One of our clients wears the same shirt nearly every time we see him (yes, it's washed). It's an Old Navy shirt from twenty years ago with an American flag on it. Is he still wearing it because he can't afford a new shirt? No, he wears it because he is content with what he has and is not trying to impress others with new fancy clothing. He even says, "They don't make shirts like they used to." He has bought a product of quality from a manufacturer he believes shares his own commitment to being . . .

8. Trusting and Trustworthy

Because the needed planning is so complex, many Midwestern Millionaires work with a team as they prepare for retirement and work through retirement. This means they trust a team to help manage what they have worked so hard to accumulate for the last forty years. That kind of trust is important, especially when the team might not understand how much this means to you and how much you have sacrificed to get to where you are.

Integrity is one of the most essential qualities a financial planning team must have when managing someone's life savings. You must find out if the advisory team you decide to work with has integrity. Ask the right questions, research the company, and search the team's personal social media pages (to see who they are when they're not in a suit and what they do when no one is watching). "How you do anything is how you do everything." This is your life savings, so who you trust to help you with it is a big decision.

Now, as promised, I will present my story about blueberries, which illustrates the Midwestern Millionaire's character traits very well.

Frozen Blueberries

I was at my parents' house one day and happened to open their deep freezer. After staring unbelievingly for half a minute, I realized the entire freezer chest was full of blueberries. The whole thing!

I asked my mother why she would do something like this, and she said: "Because they were on sale."

I definitely understand that "sale" concept. I'm the same way (family trait—the apple didn't fall far from the tree). I buy items on sale and save money when I can, because I work hard for my money, and I value it. I still had to challenge my mom, however, and press her for more information. She's in a great financial situation and wouldn't be set back by buying blueberries at full price (even in the quantity filling her freezer).

"It's the principle of the matter," she explained.

It's what she was taught throughout her years growing up. My mom came from a bigger family and was taught how to be frugal and to wisely preserve and conserve what she had. She has carried that mindset with her throughout her life. Just like almost every Midwestern Millionaire, she is naturally frugal.

What I have found after a lifetime of observing my mother's behaviors, traits, and values is that this type of money-saving purchase gives her joy. To save money on something she would have bought anyway delights her—like she's won. It is, in fact, the principle of the matter to her: Even though she can buy the blueberries at full price and not hurt financially because of it, she would rather save the money and consider it a win in her books for being frugal. I'm sure many of you reading this book share this trait.

This is the kind of Midwestern Millionaire care, attention, and diligence you want to deploy when it comes to managing and maximizing your life savings. It's the kind of attention and care we deploy for each client. That's why we work with those with Midwestern values, just like us.

Back to my mom for a moment. Sometimes I try not to encourage my mom about how well she's doing because she currently works with us at Peak Retirement Planning, Inc., as my executive assistant. It's a job she's good at and has experience with. She worked for the federal government in Columbus, Ohio for the top executives at the Defense Logistics Agency, which is a big deal. Here's the thing: I can't let her think she could retire, or I would lose a key employee. I'm joking, of course. I seriously love working with my mom. She quit her job to help me start this firm when I was twenty-five years old. That means the world to me.

People often ask what it's like working with my mom, and I tell them it's nothing new. She has been my assistant and been there for me all my life. Although she could retire, she enjoys the purpose of our mission that we have and is dedicated to serving others. Many Midwestern Millionaires also share that trait of wanting to have a purpose throughout all their years, including retirement.

Now, let's dive into the care, attention, and diligence that is needed and what Midwestern Millionaires must do now with their life savings to protect it.

2

WHY WE SERVE THE MIDWESTERN MILLIONAIRE

So why did we design a firm to serve these people? My short reason: Because they need help and recognize that fact. And because we're just like them. We're hardworking people from humble beginnings who are here to take care of those who trust us with their life savings. It seems (and is my observation) that Midwestern Millionaires have a far more complex financial picture than most of their peers in or near retirement.

I often say to them, "You don't need to keep saving more money, but you do need a better set of plans to protect the wealth you have accumulated." They know when you have over $1 million saved, you have more complex and advanced financial strategies that need to be applied. Someone with less savings can get by with more basic strategies and won't need the sophisticated strategies geared toward the Midwestern Millionaire. We'll discuss a number of these advanced strategies in this book.

We also have to understand, though, that the Midwestern Millionaires we work with have different goals and values to plan for than others. They see money in a different way. They see money not only as a way to have peace of mind and stability throughout retirement but also as a way to accomplish their purpose. Knowing how hard they worked for forty or so years to amass this wealth makes their planning much more meaningful.

As mentioned, a main reason why we attract people like this to work with our firm is because we are so similar. Who *we* are is who *our clients* are. As they say, like attracts like.

I grew up in Carroll, Ohio, a rural community outside Columbus. If you've never heard of Carroll, no worries—most haven't. I won't hold it against you. There is one traffic light (and sometimes it works). A blink-and-you-miss-it kind of town. Carroll is a farming community full of people with the Midwestern values I have set forth. I'm blessed to have been raised in such a great community with great people. Some of the best Midwestern people I know are from Carroll. I was born, raised and schooled in these Midwestern values. I was taught to work hard and to never settle for less with anything I do. All my life, I've tried hard to carry that with me.

I've done manual work for my dad since I was five years old. Working around a farm, fixing up houses, landscaping, anything that involved being pushed, challenged, and getting things done. Not all our clients do work like that, but they all can relate to the mindset it takes to be successful in tasks like that and life in general.

I was taught that trust isn't given but earned by holding true to your word and doing what you say. I was taught when doing business with others that your word is your bond—you look them in the eye, shake their hand, and make it happen.

If you know anything about business, people work with people they like and trust more readily than with strangers whose values are unclear. I think that's why we have attracted the Midwestern Millionaires, and we enjoy serving like-minded people. We work with this crowd because they acknowledge that they need specialist advice—and more than one type of specialist. They're not interested in working with a generalist.

Many advisors work with those in the accumulation phase and only specialize in investment management. They don't specialize in the other important pillars of retirement like tax and estate planning. It's like going to your family doctor to get heart surgery. Not me! I would rather have a heart surgeon who has done it many times and does it every day.

They also want every specialist available to them in one place, and they want to work with a team, not an individual. They want all their financial professionals—CERTIFIED FINANCIAL PLANNER®, certified public accountant (CPA), and attorney—working out of the same office. They want that office to also have other specialists for things like Medicare and insurance. They not only want them in one place but want them collaborating to ensure nothing is missed.

At Peak Retirement Planning, Inc., our financial planners sit in on all meetings with each professional. They make sure our clients' specific questions get specific answers and the right documents and accounts get created for them—accounts we then manage for them.

Some refer to this setup as a "family office." Working with a family office has normally only been for those who are ultra-high net worth and have saved over $30 million. This service costs $100,000 per year or more for those people. Not here. The goal at our firm is to deliver a similar service model at a lower cost. This attention to overdelivering for the client is why we have grown so much over the years. It's innovative and different from most of the big firms that only do investment management for a full fee.

We would encourage you to work with a team who specialize in working with people like you every day, whether that's us or another firm who does this type of planning. You deserve the best and should not settle for less when many generalists may charge you the same fee as a specialist.

Is a Midwestern Millionaire Wealthy?

According to the finance and investing website DQYDJ,[2] a Midwestern Millionaire is considered "wealthy." If you have a net worth over $1 million, then you are in the top 13 percent net worth in the entire country—wealthy. If you have over $3 million, then you are in the top 5 percent in the entire country.

I have to tell you a funny story about one of our clients that reveals one big character trait of all the Midwestern Millionaires. In an early meeting, I asked him, "How does it feel to be rich?" He was the definition of the Midwestern Millionaire and had $2.5 million saved for retirement.

Well, you know what? He got upset with me. "Joe, please!" he said. "I'm not rich. That's a different type of person. I don't do things that rich people do." I told him he was right, but from a net-worth standpoint, he was among the top group of wealthy people in the country. I agreed not to call him rich anymore, but I couldn't help but make him understand that he had significant wealth compared to his peers and would therefore be considered a wealthy American.

---

2   PK, "Average, Median, Top 1%, and all United States Net Worth Percentiles," DQYDJ, accessed July 9, 2024, https://dqydj.com/net-worth-percentiles/.

Often this crowd doesn't realize the scope of wealth they have achieved until we meet with them and share how well they've done. They find it hard to believe they're wealthy. All they've known and done is work hard and be a diligent saver over time, putting their heads down and doing what was needed.

Just because they've done well in accumulating money does not mean no other action is needed—and they know this. They know they have to take action, but they come to us so they take the right action and protect their wealth to the highest degree possible. Remember, Luke 12:48 tells us that from those to whom much is given, much is required.

WHAT MUST A MIDWESTERN MILLIONAIRE DO?

Midwestern Millionaires have accumulated. They need a way to protect and maximize the wealth they have. They know they need and will have to create an advanced plan. Not a cookie-cutter plan; their situation is unique being in the top 13 percent of wealth accumulators in the United States.

I tell them their "plan" is really five plans in one. Our firm calls them the "5 pillars" of retirement planning: tax, investment, income, healthcare, and estate planning. The best financial plan must solve a range of issues in each of those categories.

As you read these pages, you will notice how the pillars and plans intersect. And most importantly, to protect your wealth in the best way, you will notice how each plan must rest on a strong tax-efficient foundation.

Ten Actions

There might be 5 pillars (and we return to them throughout the book), but here are ten actions within the pillars that Midwestern Millionaires need to take to protect their wealth:

1. Save through Tax Planning

Many Midwestern Millionaires have the potential to save hundreds of thousands of dollars through tax planning. Most of these people have their money in tax-deferred investments like 401(k)s and individual retirement accounts (IRAs), which will require them to pay taxes when they withdraw their money.

By doing proactive tax planning (discussed in virtually every chapter of this book, so keep reading!) and correctly implementing the strategies we discuss in this book, you could create massive tax savings. That leaves more money in your pocket. Our firm uses over one hundred tax-saving strategies, and we leverage software, calculators, and reports to support our recommendations and your decisions.

2. Reduce Required Minimum Distributions

Is it ever a good thing when the government forces you to do something? The tax authorities have a thing called required minimum distributions (RMDs), which obligate you to withdraw money from your tax-deferred investments starting at age seventy-three, or if you were born in 1960 or after, then you must start taking it out at seventy-five.

For Midwestern Millionaires, these RMDs can force them into paying more taxes throughout their retirement if they don't plan for this. (Read more about this in chapter 5.)

3. Reduce Tax on Social Security

When you receive your Social Security benefit, it can either be tax-free, 85 percent taxable, or somewhere in between.

We work with many of our clients to avoid what we call the "Social Security tax torpedo." This is a situation where most of their Social Security is taxable when it could have been avoided. This is an especially big concern for those who have a higher expected RMD coming in the future. Plan so you keep more of your Social Security in your pocket and turn over less to Uncle Sam. (Read more about Social Security planning and this torpedo in chapter 7.)

4. Reduce Healthcare Costs

Reducing healthcare costs can involve not only planning for long-term care, which is a big concern for retirees, but also planning for IRMAA. The income-related monthly adjustment amount is an increased cost for Medicare Part B and Part D for those who have a higher income in retirement.

This issue of higher income and IRMAA is something we often see with Midwestern Millionaires because they've been diligent savers. This means those who have done the right thing and saved have to pay more for Medicare Part B and D. I don't like that concept. We'll talk about how to avoid these higher Medicare tiers so you can pay your fair share into Medicare and no more.

By the way, you don't get better Medicare benefits by paying more. Every Medicare enrollee gets the same benefits. I would say this is important to plan for unless you would like to donate money above and beyond what they tell you to pay. I haven't seen anyone do that yet. (Read more about Aunt IRMAA and healthcare planning in chapter 8.)

5. Be Tax Efficient with Income Planning

How are you going to get a paycheck for the rest of your life now that you're no longer working? Which investments do you plan to pull your retirement income from? What will you do if the market is down?

Those are key questions to ask and answer, then plan for when it comes to income planning. If you're trying to maximize your income and stretch your life savings further, you must plan for the tax impact when taking income from your investments, Social Security, and other sources of income.

When it comes to tax-efficient income planning, I love a quote from Robert Kiyosaki's book *Rich Dad, Poor Dad*:

"It's not how much money you make. It's how much money you keep."[3]

If you take out $100,000 but only keep $90,000, how much do you have to spend? The $90,000, of course. So how can we take out $100,000 and spend $100,000? Paying $10,000 less in taxes every year seems intriguing, I'm sure. I'll show you how it can be done and how realistic it is to decrease your lifetime tax bill and increase your lifetime income. (Read more about income planning in chapter 4.)

6. Be Tax Efficient with Charitable Giving

The more you have, the more opportunity you have to be generous. If you give $5,000 or more to charities every year without using any charitable strategies, you could be leaving money on the table (that is, you didn't get a tax benefit from giving that money). If this is you, there are many strategies you can start using or plan to use throughout retirement. We'll discuss how to either give more to the charities you love or keep more in your pocket. (Read more on this topic in chapters 9 and 10.)

7. Prepare for the "Widow's Penalty"

The widow's penalty is one of my least favorite parts of the tax code and usually puts the Midwestern Millionaire in a tough financial position if they haven't planned for this. It

---

[3] Robert T. Kiyosaki, *Rich Dad Poor Dad* (Plata Publishing, 2011).

severely penalizes those who lose a spouse, so it's really a "widow" and a "widower" penalty.

Two key things happen here. First, you lose one of the Social Security benefits (but you do get to keep the higher of the two). Second, your tax rates go from the lower "married filing jointly" rates to the higher "single" rates. This could cause you to pay nearly double the amount of taxes after losing a spouse. (Read more about this in chapter 9.)

8. Create the Right Legacy through Estate Planning

Planning helps ensure that when you die, Uncle Sam isn't a primary beneficiary of your hard-earned life savings. You should be protecting your life savings through proper and early estate planning. This will ensure your money is left to the loved ones or charities you wish to designate and in the most efficient ways. (Read more about this in chapter 9.)

Estate planning involves special types of tax planning (with a financial planner who is a tax specialist) and advanced planning with trusts and key estate planning documents (with an estate attorney). This works best when the professionals collaborate.

9. Be Aware of Estate Taxes

To further touch on the power of planning for taxes and estate in tandem, we must always examine the dreaded estate tax. This tax is least planned for because most people aren't concerned about it "right now." As time progresses, however, many Midwestern Millionaires need to make sure they're aware of and alert for estate taxes since the rules will likely change. This tax has been as high as 50 percent if you had over $1 million net worth in the early 2000s. That would affect all Midwestern Millionaires if that happened again. (We'll discuss this in chapter 9.)

10. Have a Purpose

Plan for what your money can be purposefully used for. Midwestern Millionaires are the best savers but the worst spenders. We have to encourage them to spend money, as odd as that may seem in our consumption-driven society. If you don't want to spend your money, you should decide where you want your money to go. As you know, you can't take it with you.

You need to consider the impact of leaving your money to someone or some organization. Will it go to your kids? Will it go to your grandkids to set them up for success? Do you have a beloved charity? With proper planning, you'll know if you should start giving now. (Read more about this in chapter 10.)

These ten actions are some of the planning topics the Midwestern Millionaire must and does consider.

Protect and Maximize

Taken together, the 5 pillars of retirement planning and ten of the actions that fall within those pillars involve protecting and maximizing your wealth. Having a master tax plan, but also being tax wise for your income plan, investment plan, healthcare plan, and estate plan, means you have not only protected your wealth but maximized what your money can do for you.

To emulate the money-wise Midwestern Millionaire, you need to take care every step of the way, and with each pillar of planning, you can optimize your tax picture. Formalize the 5 pillars in writing and review them with your advisors regularly. Keep more of your money to spend or share as you wish.

If you would like to learn more about our holistic and comprehensive approach, get my book *Peak Retirement: The 5 Pillars to Protect Your Wealth and Live the Retirement You Deserve*.[4] It goes into even more detail about the 5 pillars of retirement planning.

---

[4] Joe F. Schmitz Jr., *Peak Retirement: The 5 Pillars to Protect Your Wealth and Live the Retirement You Deserve* (Expert Press, 2024), available on Amazon at https://www.amazon.com/Peak-Retirement-Pillars-Protect-Deserve-ebook/dp/B0CW14N7CB.

We'll explore this idea of being "tax smart" in the next chapter. As I've said, taxes are a core issue to address as you dive into each of the above planning points.

4

TAXES—ARE YOU OVERPAYING?

Ask anyone in our office. Ask any of our clients. Ask any of my family and friends. Ask anyone who has heard me speak on TV, radio, YouTube, or podcasts, or has read my books or my articles featured in Kiplinger. As you've certainly already deduced and will read in the coming pages as well, I have strong opinions when it comes to taxes. I don't deny it.

My opinions are so strong, in fact, that I wrote a book called *I Hate Taxes*.[5] That title caught a lot of attention. The book became a national bestseller on Amazon and really put our firm on the map. We've had people from across the country contact us to work with our team after reading

---

5   Joe F. Schmitz Jr., *I Hate Taxes: Lower Your Taxes, Own Your Retirement* (Expert Press, 2023), available on Amazon at https://www.amazon.com/Hate-Taxes-Lower-Your-Retirement-ebook/dp/B0CKXZMJMR.

the book. Why? Because I'm not alone in hating taxes. Midwestern Millionaires also hate taxes.

I always want to underscore this fact: I don't mind paying taxes, and I think some taxes are good. I will without hesitation pay my *legitimately fair share* of taxes. I love our military, first responders, roads, parks, schools, and libraries, to name a few. I will always be on time with my filing and payment.

So here are my thoughts on the subject:

1. I don't like giving control to Uncle Sam about how much of my hard-earned money is fair to pay.

2. I don't feel the government is the best steward of all our tax dollars.

3. I don't agree with the concept of "the more you make, the more you pay." I don't think it's in the Midwestern Millionaire's or any American's best interests to be penalized with more taxes simply because they've done so well earning, saving, and being diligent with their money all their life.

And because they can't understand and leverage the US tax code on their own, they are overtaxed, while the person who doesn't work hard and wasn't diligent is rewarded and gets to pay less. Does it make sense to disincentivize hard work and smart money management?

I find that most Midwestern Millionaires hate taxes too. But they live an honest life and want to find legitimate ways to not overpay during their retirement years. We help them achieve that. We do it all day, every day, for people just like them.

Tax Planning

Tax planning is the key to a sound retirement plan, and as you can see in our 5 pillars of retirement planning image on page 4, tax planning is the central, most prominent pillar. As the image suggests, taxes should be at the top of your planning list and the first financial analysis you complete.

As I've already stated (and repeat daily), taxes are a consideration in all your planning: income planning, investment planning, healthcare planning, and estate planning. Tax efficiency is involved in each pillar. Unfortunately, taxes seem to be *the least* planned for. Mostly because the average American doesn't understand our tax system and do not take the time to learn it themselves or get a team who understands.

For most of the Midwestern Millionaires we work with, taxes will be the biggest expense for them during their retirement years. And that's exactly why you must start with tax planning and proactively update your plan on a regular basis. This is because tax rules and amounts change every year. If you don't have a tax plan, it's going to be hard to plan for the other four pillars. Why? Because, again, the other four pillars play off and depend upon the tax plan. Let's discuss how this works by diving into the effects that tax planning has on each pillar.

Investment Planning

Investment planning is an important one among our 5 pillars. If you get a 10 percent rate of return on your investments, that's great. But what if the share of taxes taken reduces your investment to a net 7 percent return? That means fewer dollars in your income plan. If you have nonqualified investments, you must understand the impacts of capital gains and dividends that can cause returns to lag behind if not managed with tax efficiency.

Income Planning

If you plan to take from your investments for income, what will the tax impact be on your income? If you take $100,000 out, will you keep $100,000? It's about how much you keep, not how much you take.

When it comes to your Social Security, do you know if it's fully taxable and forcing you into higher tax brackets? Tax planning will make that clear. More tax on your Social Security benefit means you'll have less to spend in retirement.

Healthcare Planning

Without looking at the tax issues, will you have enough cash for healthcare expenses? What if you must take $100,000 from your IRA for a nursing home? What will that do to your income and tax picture? Will your income become higher with RMDs and force you to pay more for IRMAA?

Estate Planning

Will taxes eat up your ability to leave the legacy you choose? If you don't plan for the taxes, you could be making Uncle Sam a beneficiary of your wealth. Through efficient tax planning, you can leave more to your beneficiaries. You must plan for things like the ten-year rule for inherited IRAs, step-up cost basis, estate tax, and others.

By starting with tax planning and then moving into the planning for the other four pillars—the investment, income, healthcare, and estate plans—you're taking what we call a "holistic approach." Our firm is on a mission: to help our clients understand the need for and benefits of tax planning. By planning efficiently, you can keep more of what you've earned.

Legislative Risk: Is the Tax Code Written in Pencil?

A big concern of the Midwestern Millionaire is the future outlook on taxes. Most think taxes will increase in the future because of our country's enormous debt, tax rates being at an all-time low, and government overspending. I have strong convictions and beliefs on this topic. If you ever hear or see me, I'm probably discussing taxes and our nation's current economic state. At the time of writing this book, our country has over $35 trillion in national debt[6] (and it's growing every day). Have you ever seen that number spelled out? That's a large number. It's the number thirty-five followed by twelve zeros:

$$\$35,000,000,000,000$$

Many have difficulties wrapping their head around "just" $10 million or the jackpot amounts of any lottery game—and this debt is many multiples larger. What must happen if we want to cover this debt crisis? There are many things that can happen, but it comes down to two key points: The government can either spend less or raise more revenue.

---

6   US Debt Clock.org is a continuously running measure of the nation's debt, accessed September 7, 2024, https://www.usdebtclock.org/.

Do we think they will spend less? They could, but I haven't seen it happen in recent times, and I don't expect it to start now—regardless of who's in office. How can they raise more revenue? The obvious answer is to raise taxes, which most people expect to happen.

There are many other ways, however, that the government can raise revenue, including increasing taxes in more ways than just federal tax rates on individual and business income. Let's consider a few of those ways to give you an idea:

1. Make Medicare premiums more expensive (the federal government banks them)

2. Reduce Social Security benefits (the federal government won't have to pay out as much)

3. Reduce the estate tax limit (so more people pay that tax)

4. Get rid of the stepped-up cost basis on assets when you pass away (a tax provision that currently adjusts the value of an inherited asset to its fair market value at the time of the owner's death; it can result in significant tax savings for heirs, especially for assets that have substantially appreciated over time.)

The Congressional Budget Office issues a report to discuss the practical changes they could make to shrink our country's debt burden. The common theme among these changes is to raise revenue using the above and other means. All these approaches negatively affect us and take more money out of our pockets and put it into the government's pockets. The good news is that I will continue to remind you of this and that proactive planning can set you up to be less affected.

You've probably heard the statement over and over (and most often during election campaigns) that the government is looking to tax the rich. Well, they always have and always will. Be aware, when the government says "rich," they mean you—the Midwestern Millionaire. The authorities are continually trying to change the rules that affect high-net-worth individuals and others with high incomes.

You don't need a high income from working or earned income to be considered part of this category. If you're sixty years old with $3 million in your IRA, that amount could double to $6 million by the time you're seventy-five, when it's time to take out your RMD. In this scenario, the rules could force you to take $240,000 from your IRA the year you're seventy-five. That, added to your Social Security income and potentially a pension, is a high income, if you ask the IRS, and you pay taxes on it regardless of whether or not you're working at the time. Food for thought—and serious planning now.

TAXES—ARE YOU OVERPAYING?

Has anyone ever told you that you would be in a lower tax situation in retirement? That may be true for most people, but it's not the case for diligent Midwestern Millionaire savers. Remember your situation is unique. Most Midwestern Millionaires say they're paying similar taxes, if not more, in retirement.

What Does History Tell Us About Tax Rates?

Right now, as I write this in 2025, our tax rates are among the lowest we've seen since World War II, which ended in 1945. Look at the following chart, which shows the highest historical tax brackets for each year during the entire lifetime of the US federal tax rates:

Taxing The Rich: How America's Marginal Tax Rate Evolved

Historic highest marginal income tax rates in the U.S.*

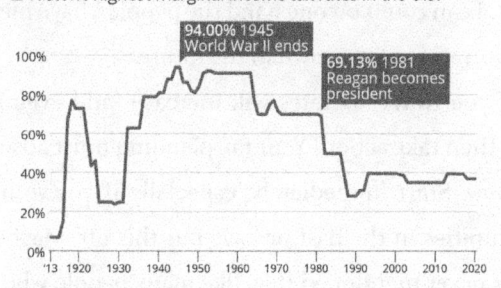

- 94.00% 1945 World War II ends
- 69.13% 1981 Reagan becomes president

* Marginal tax rate is the highest tax rate paid on someone's income and only applies to income over a certain level. - e.g. earnings above $200,000 in 1960 were taxed at 90%.
Source: Tax Policy Center

statista

Source: "Taxing The Rich: How America's Marginal Tax Rate Evolved" (https://www.statista.com/chart/16782/historic-marginal-income-tax-rates/) by Niall McCarthy is licensed under CC BY-ND 4.0 (https://creativecommons.org/licenses/by-nd/4.0/).

Can you believe the highest tax bracket of all time was 94 percent? That makes today's 37 percent look like a bargain.

You know what I like to say about this? Taxes are now *on sale*. Grabbing the advantage of this rate is better than any blueberry sale my mother could ever find.

The chart clearly shows us that tax rates have been much higher in the past. So if tax rates are low now, and they have been significantly higher in the past, *and* our legislators are looking for ways to resolve our big debt crisis, what do you think will happen in the immediate and longer-term future?

You have the right to believe what you want when it comes to expectations of future tax rates—especially since none of us know what will happen. After all, the tax code is written in pencil, and our legislators can make tax rules and rates into whatever they want. Whatever your opinion on the subject, I can count on one hand the people I have met who think tax rates will go down in the future.

If you think tax rates will increase (and even if you don't), then take action! Your tax planning must absolutely start now. Start immediately, especially if you've missed opportunities in the past or have put this off. Maybe your advisor never mentioned this, like many people who come to us say.

You can't change the past, but you can change the future. It's never too late.

5

WHICH BUCKETS HOLD YOUR LIFE SAVINGS?

I'm a big believer in keeping things simple when it comes to financial planning. My mentor, Kathy Gilliland, who was a financial planner for forty years and is now retired, always told me to keep it simple. She's the one responsible for getting me into the financial planning industry. I owe a lot of my success to her. If it weren't for her, I may not have found my passion and purpose.

She always told me to keep everything at a fourth-grade level when explaining financial planning topics. She always emphasized that not everyone has studied financial planning or has ever planned a retirement. Few have the credentials or the interest that I have. She said people just want to know what they need to know and to make sure their financial house is in order.

That's why I always make the books I write and content I produce easy to read and understand while also talking about advanced topics and strategies that are important to know. We do this by using simple terms and stories. We like to explain financial topics through the use of "buckets."

I'm going to explain three different tax buckets where your assets may be held. I'll share where most Midwestern Millionaires have their money, and where we may want to look to start shifting some of our money.

Taxable   Tax Deferred   Tax Free

The Taxable Bucket

The first bucket is called the taxable bucket. This bucket consists of money you have, on which you have already paid tax. Your responsibility now is to pay tax on any growth you see in this account ongoing.

These investments are also known as nonqualified or nonretirement investment accounts. It is the gains or profits that are taxed at either capital gain rates or ordinary income tax rates that depend on the vehicle where the money is held.

The investments that may be taxed at capital gains rates might include your house or a business, a stock, a mutual fund, an exchange-traded fund you've had for a long time in an individual or jointly owned brokerage account, or maybe it's one named to a trust.

What's unique about these investments is they have a special and lower tax bracket. For example, you could pay 0 percent on long-term capital gains (on investments held for longer than a year) if your taxable income is $96,700 or less in 2025. Most Midwestern Millionaires find themselves in the 15 percent capital gains bracket. This means if they own a stock that they bought for $10,000 and now it's worth $110,000, they will have to pay capital gains tax at a rate of 15 percent, or $15,000 in taxes on the gain of $100,000.

There are ways to reduce this tax through specific tax strategies. In the next chapter, I will present five of the strategies we use that apply, whether they're selling rental properties or highly appreciated stocks or assets.

With this taxable investment, we want people to be aware of what we call "tax location." If you hold a protected investment like a certificate of deposit, annuity, money market, or a treasury note, then you'll change the tax treatment from capital gains to ordinary income. We're not a big fan of this and will try to prevent this move with clients, if we can, so they can continue to have the preferential tax treatment of capital gains.

Here's how that might look. If you're in the 12 percent ordinary income tax bracket, then you're in the 0 percent capital gains bracket. Which one would you rather have? And if you're in the 22 percent or 24 percent ordinary income tax bracket, then you could be in the 15 percent capital gains bracket. Again, which would you prefer?

Not managing this up front can significantly increase the amount of taxes you pay over time. Especially knowing right now that if you pass away, there is a stepped-up basis on taxable investments that are under capital gains. "Stepped up" means your beneficiaries may pay no taxes on these investments at that time, which could make this investment part of the tax-free bucket if used correctly.

The next bucket holds assets you have not yet paid tax on but will at some point.

The Tax-Deferred Bucket

The second bucket is the tax-deferred bucket. This is where the majority of Americans have their money saved. Examples of tax-deferred accounts are the 401(k), IRA, 403(b), 457, Thrift Savings Plan. This is basically any of these retirement accounts mentioned or any accounts you've funded through your employer.

When you put $10,000 into this account, you get a tax savings today because you've reduced your income on your tax return this year by $10,000. That's a great feeling—for today. When you pull the money out in the future, however, when your investment has now perhaps grown to $100,000 due to the profits earned on it, you now have to pay taxes on the whole $100,000. That's because the IRS is capturing the tax due on the initial $10,000 *and* on the $90,000 in profits.

Let's look at the big picture: You reduced your income and your taxes one year back then by saving $10,000 into such an account, only to pay tax now on $100,000. Is that a good deal? Well, it could have been. A big part of it is what tax rate you saved on when you put the money in and which tax rate you pay when you take the money out.

We'll talk further about this.

The Retirement-Tax Time Bomb

You may have heard others calling this tax-deferred bucket the "retirement-tax time bomb." They call it this because your tax burden grows over time in this bucket, and at some point in retirement, when you either take out money on your own or the government requires you to take out a certain amount of that money (the RMD), you could end up paying more in taxes at unknown tax rates.

As we've already discussed, people expect tax rates in the future to go up. But years ago, when you saved that $10,000, you couldn't predict—no one could have or can—how much gain, if any, the $10,000 would earn and what your future tax rate on the amount might be.

I always joke that tax-deferred investment accounts are jointly owned with the IRS. You don't know how much your share is until you've paid those taxes. The problem with this joint ownership is you don't get to decide the amount of your share versus the amount of Uncle Sam's. Good ole Uncle Sam decides because—the tax code being written in pencil—he can make tax rates whatever he wants, whenever he wants.

Right now, you're probably thinking you made a bad decision by saving most of your retirement savings in this tax-deferred bucket. But wait! This is where I come in and make you feel better. I would argue that if you have put money in this bucket over the years, then you may have made the right decision.

Remember, tax rates right now are among the lowest in history. If you contributed to a 401(k) in 1981 and were in the highest tax bracket then, you would have saved 69 percent in tax that year on your contribution. On the other side, if you paid tax on that investment today, you would have paid only 37 percent if you were in the highest bracket. Frankly, I would much rather *save* at 69 percent and *pay* at 37 percent, and I'm sure you would too. That's what shows me that you may have made the right decision.

But in order to make sure you have made the right decision, consult a professional who will run the numbers for you. You may want to pay your taxes on those tax-deferred funds now, at our current lower rate. That's what we see many Midwestern Millionaires wanting to do. If you wait, the tax rates could potentially go up in the future, especially when you're forced to take the money out, which we'll discuss next.

More on the Tax-Deferred Bucket

Let's discuss these tax-deferred investments a bit more, since it's a tax story that unfolds over decades. Yes, *over decades.*

Required minimum distributions (RMDs) are related to tax-deferred investment accounts like the 401(k). As I stated earlier, the IRS requires all those holding tax-deferred accounts to make a specified minimum annual withdrawal of funds from those accounts and pay the taxes due on the withdrawal. They tell you when you must start doing it and for how many years. Retirees with $1 million or more in tax-deferred investments fear RMDs—and rightly so. Here's where we come in and say, "Let go of the fear with proper tax planning."

Now let's dive into more detail of what this can look like. What follows is an RMD calculator we use for our clients to give them an idea of what this looks like.

PEAK RETIREMENT PLANNING, INC.

RMD Calculator

Estimated Rate of Return

6.00%

Client Account Balance
$ 1,000,000

Client Birthdate
1951

Add Second Client

[Calculate]

Client RMD

Year	Age	Account Balance	RMD
2024	73	$1,060,000.00	$40,068.00
2025	74	$1,081,127.92	$42,488.33
2026	75	$1,100,957.97	$44,808.99
2027	76	$1,119,517.92	$47,243.66
2028	77	$1,136,610.72	$49,669.89
2029	78	$1,152,157.28	$52,423.16
2030	79	$1,165,718.17	$55,255.04
2031	80	$1,177,090.92	$58,383.71
2032	81	$1,185,829.64	$61,168.81
2033	82	$1,192,119.28	$64,493.65
2034	83	$1,195,283.16	$67,533.50
2035	84	$1,195,414.65	$71,246.71
2036	85	$1,191,618.01	$74,476.13
2037	86	$1,184,170.40	$77,918.41
2038	87	$1,172,627.10	$81,497.58
2039	88	$1,156,597.29	$84,431.60
2040	89	$1,136,495.63	$88,192.06
2041	90	$1,111,201.78	$91,118.55
2042	91	$1,081,288.23	$94,072.08
2043	92	$1,046,449.12	$96,901.19
2044	93	$1,006,520.81	$99,746.21
2045	94	$961,181.07	$101,212.37
2046	95	$911,566.83	$102,460.11
2047	96	$857,053.12	$102,140.49
2048	97	$800,837.03	$102,747.39
2049	98	$739,975.02	$101,376.58
2050	99	$676,914.35	$99,574.10
2051	100	$611,980.66	$95,652.58
2052	101	$547,307.77	$91,236.21
2053	102	$483,435.86	$86,341.64
2054	103	$420,919.87	$80,984.98
2055	104	$360,330.98	$73,543.55
2056	105	$303,994.67	$66,088.44
2057	106	$252,180.60	#N/A

WHICH BUCKETS HOLD YOUR LIFE SAVINGS?

Let's say someone has $1 million in tax-deferred accounts, and as you can see in the chart above, they are seventy-three years old. This means their RMD—and let me remind you that this is their mandatory minimum withdrawal or they face a stiff penalty—is $40,068 for that first RMD year.

They can't go out and spend the whole amount, as it is the gross amount only. First, they need to pay tax on that mandatory $40,068 they have to withdraw. The net amount after tax is what is available for them to spend. But how much will that be if you're sixty-three years old today, planning your retirement income, and don't have any idea what the tax rates will look like in ten years?

Didn't everyone tell you that you were going to be in a lower tax bracket in retirement? Remember when we discussed that earlier? Unfortunately, you're likely to find yourself in the same tax bracket or in a higher one in retirement due to Social Security now being taxable (it didn't used to be) and with your RMD amounts. Add in a potential pension, and good luck being in a lower tax bracket throughout retirement.

Let me go back to my crystal-ball questions:

- Do we think tax rates will be higher or lower in the future?

- Do we want to force ourselves to take out this much money and pay potentially higher tax rates in the future?

Here's another piece of news: The RMD amount goes up over time. You see it clearly on the above chart. At age ninety-five (if healthy and Lord willing), this person must withdraw $102,460. And pay tax on it.

You may only have to take out about 3.78 percent of your tax-deferred balance at the age of seventy-three, but if you were to reach ninety-five, your RMD percentage will be 11.24 percent. Thus, the older you get, the worse this tax-due scenario can get, especially if your investments continue to grow over time.

Planning against all of the above comes in the form of a popular strategy we're seeing Midwestern Millionaires implement right now: the Roth conversion. And yes, it's directly connected to that Roth IRA account you've certainly heard about.

We'll talk about this strategy in the next chapter, but first, let's discuss the tax-free bucket and how that plays a part here.

The Tax-Free Bucket

The third bucket is the tax-free bucket.

I was on a radio show with call-in questions from listeners during which someone called in and asked me to share everything I knew about tax-free investments. I'm sure the listeners were on high alert to hear me speak on the topic, but I had to pause. I asked the caller (with a little chuckle) if he wanted me to be on the air all day, or if he wanted me to give him the Cliffs Notes version of a popular tax-free investment that is also most popular with the Midwestern Millionaire.

That's what I'll share here.

The Roth IRA

Now, about that Roth IRA. First, don't believe you can escape taxes altogether. The Roth IRA isn't completely tax-free. You have to have paid taxes on your money before putting it into the Roth IRA.

The advantage to you is that, contrary to an ordinary IRA, the investments the Roth IRA account holds grow *tax-free*. In other words, before you put in $10,000, you have to have paid taxes on it. But if that $10,000 grows to $100,000, you pay no tax when you take out any portion of your $100,000.

I always ask people, "If you had a magic wand, where would you like to have all your money?" As you can imagine, they all say the Roth IRA. Unfortunately, 75 percent of Americans don't have a Roth IRA account. That means only one-quarter of us have a Roth IRA.[7] Why don't more people have Roth IRAs?

First, there are three restrictive criteria:

1. If you make too much money, you can't contribute.

2. You have to have earned income to contribute.

3. There is only so much you can contribute per year.

Also, the Roth IRA hasn't been around forever. It didn't get signed into law until 1997, and the Roth 401(k) didn't start until 2006. It took employers even longer to offer Roth 401(k)s to employees, and some have just started to offer this option recently. Those Midwestern Millionaires who had started saving and investing long before that were already into their habits and often missed the Roth opportunity.

---

[7] Chris Neiger, "Stats Show This Many Americans Are Missing Out on Roth IRA Contributions," The Ascent: A Motley Fool Service, Fool.com, March 11, 2024, accessed September 7, 2024, https://www.fool.com/the-ascent/buying-stocks/articles/stats-show-this-many-americans-are-missing-out-on-roth-ira-contributions/.

So you may be thinking you've got all the excuses in the world to not do a Roth IRA.

Again, wait! That's where I come in and share with you a strategy you may want to look into: the Roth conversion. This is one of the most popular tax-planning strategies we're seeing right now. Many people who are in or near retirement are taking advantage of this strategy before tax rates go up. If you haven't implemented this strategy or you haven't looked at it, I would highly encourage you to write this one down. The majority of our clients are doing it right now, but make sure you're doing your due diligence to see how it could work for you.

I'll explain how you do a Roth conversion in the next chapter, along with several other strategies of potential interest to you. This is where you move money from the tax-deferred bucket to the tax-free bucket.

Note that I may have confused you when I said earlier that there are a number of limits on an individual's ability to fund a Roth (a.k.a. to make contributions). Remember that *contributions* and *conversions* are two different actions and have different rules. Since 2010, we've been able to do Roth conversions without any limits. The only requirement is to pay the taxes at the time of conversion.

6

ADVANCED STRATEGIES FOR THE TAX BUCKETS

As promised, I will share the advanced tax-saving strategies for the taxable bucket, and then we'll discuss the Roth conversion strategy and several others.

Here are the five advanced tax-saving strategies for the taxable bucket:

1. Installment Sale

A pair of strategies you can look into is an installment sale or the slightly more complex deferred sales trust.[8] The goal of both strategies is to defer capital gains taxes. You stretch your capital gains over two or more years. You could absorb

---

[8] Carl E. Sera, "Section 453 Deferred Sales Trust: Simplified and Explained," Sera Capital, April 11, 2023, https://seracapital.com/deferred-sales-trust/section-453-deferred-sales-trust-simplified-and-explained/; "1031 Exchange Services," Exeter, accessed July 2024, https://www.exeterco.com/deferred_sales_trust.

half the gain one year and absorb the other half the next year, as an example.

Why would you do this? Because you could find yourself in the 0 percent bracket if you did it over two years or more. Or maybe you can keep yourself in the 15 percent bracket instead of going into the 20 percent capital gains bracket.

2. Opportunity Zone

A tax-saving real estate strategy is the opportunity zone. As of 2024, there are 8,764 opportunity zones in the United States. These opportunity zones were established as part of the 2017 Tax Cuts and Jobs Act and are designed to spur economic development and job creation in economically distressed communities.[9]

This strategy allows you to invest in eligible economically depressed communities while getting tax benefits.

3. Donor-Advised Fund

Another strategy we look at with Midwestern Millionaire clients who have highly appreciated assets and who are charitably minded is a donor-advised fund (DAF). A DAF is a charitable giving vehicle that allows donors to make tax-deductible contributions to a fund managed by a public charity.

---

9   https://opportunityzones.hud.gov, accessed November 2024.

ADVANCED STRATEGIES FOR THE TAX BUCKETS

You can take the stock and donate it to a DAF, and you pay no tax on the capital gains. You can also itemize deductions because your charitable contribution could be higher in that year.

Go back to that $10,000 stock purchase and its $100,000 gain. If you donated the net stock to the DAF, that $15,000 of tax you would have paid is now zero. You also get a full $110,000 itemized deduction on top of all the other itemized deductions you could have.

The DAF approach allows you to layer other tax strategies on top of it, such as a Roth conversion or selling other investments to offset. This is a tax-efficient way to give to charities, and it's especially useful for those with highly appreciated investments. Some of our clients who don't have appreciated assets still take advantage of a DAF to bunch charitable deductions in one year to take advantage of itemized deductions that year, and then take advantage of the higher standard deduction each year thereafter.

4. Charitable Remainder Trust

Another strategy we look into with clients is the "charitable remainder trust" (CRT). This can be used for those who are charitable minded or not.

Say you're selling a rental property. You could put the property into a CRT before you sell it. Doing so will not only allow you to get a big tax deduction now but also allow you to get income from this type of trust for your lifetime. Anything left in the trust would go to your designated charity when you pass away.

You may be asking how this strategy is beneficial for someone who isn't charitably minded. The capital gains tax is deferred. You get tax-exempt growth. Reduced estate taxes, lifetime income, and asset protection round out the benefits to you of a CRT.[10] These benefits could outweigh the amount left to the charity, give you more, and give the IRS less. The question is whether you would rather have a charity or government get your money.

There's another layer to this strategy in which the children still receive the value of the assets when you put it into the CRT, you still get an income, and the charity still gets the rest. Who's left out? Uncle Sam! Everyone wins besides him. This is what we do with our clients since they don't want to leave family out.

5. Tax-Loss Harvesting

We also like to do tax-loss harvesting with our clients' investments. Many of our clients come to us with large amounts not only in tax-deferred investments but also in taxable investments that they have owned for a long time and that have done very well.

---

10   Ali Katz, "Donate to a Charitable Remainder Trust for Tax and Income Benefits," Personal Family Lawyer, accessed July 2024, https://personalfamilylawyer.com/articles/donate-appreciated-assets-to-charity-instead-of-selling-outright-for-tax-and-income-benefits-using-a-charitable-remainder-trust.

That's a great thing as far as their saving habit goes, but a bad thing when it comes to tax planning. Every year we look at ways to sell off gains and offset them with losses to improve their tax picture and get their portfolio invested in a more tax-efficient manner.

An example of this is Exxon stock. Say it's down, so we would sell it and buy Shell stock so we don't have to worry about the wash-sale rule. We're still able to participate in any upside the stock will likely see as it comes back up. We saw this used after COVID-19 when the oil industry stocks lost over 50 percent of their value (although the value has come up quite a bit since then).

These five strategies are great to consider for your taxable bucket. Now let's move on to the tax-deferred bucket for some strategies there.

Roth Conversions

In tax planning, we never forget the Roth IRA, and a Roth conversion is a popular strategy in tax planning right now for the Midwestern Millionaire. This strategy is simple at its core: You shift money from your tax-deferred bucket into a Roth IRA. When doing this, you have to pay taxes right away on the amount you have shifted or "converted."

The question for you becomes, "Do you want to pay the tax now, or do you want to pay the tax later?" We must pay it at some point. For many, the answer is a definite "Now, please," because they assume their tax rate will be higher in the future, as we've discussed.

Before answering for our clients, though, we do an analysis. Our tax rates are low now, so you must act now to take advantage of the opportunity before the window closes and tax rates go up. Yes, that's true. But don't act without knowledge, and don't guess. Our team doesn't make guesses with our clients' hard-earned life savings.

We often get asked, "How much should I convert? Should it be everything?" You could convert everything if you wanted to. There are no amount limits on a Roth conversion. But we don't recommend converting everything at once.

Here's why:

- If you have $1 million in your tax-deferred investment accounts, as an example, converting all of it in one year may force you into the highest tax bracket, which will force other taxes and penalties.

- If you convert strategically over a certain number of years, you may not have to worry about as painful of a tax bite.

Trying to decide the optimal amount to convert into a Roth can be difficult. Don't be fooled into believing it's as easy as converting up to the next tax bracket (and I warn against this as it's the most common error I see).

Figuring out the most tax-efficient way to convert is why an expert analysis of your financial situation is recommended first. You and your tax professional must analyze your situation now and what you expect your situation to be in the future. You must also be aware of state taxes, capital gains taxes, the impact to your Social Security taxes, the impact to Medicare premiums for part B and D (the IRMAA we discussed), net investment income tax, the alternative minimum tax, and many other credits and deductions that may apply to your unique situation.

Again, I caution you. You may be great at math. You may love numbers. But this is not a DIY project: Even the experts must use advanced software, perform complex calculations, examine tax law again, and consult the most recent legislative reports to maximize this decision. We see too many people who guess, and although they're able to get the Roth conversion done, they may have lingering doubts about whether it was done in the most efficient and mistake-free manner.

You want to be careful of converting too much too quickly. Don't end up paying more taxes than you would have to in the future. Conversely, be wary of converting so little that you end up leaving lower tax rates on the table that you may not see again.

Qualified Charitable Distributions

Many Midwestern Millionaires like to support charitable organizations that work in areas of interest to them and share their values. If your goal is to give money to charities throughout your retirement, then the qualified charitable distribution (QCD) is a strategy you'll want to remember.

Since the QCD strategy is connected to your IRA, you can start contributing to a charity at the age of seventy and a half. This is when you can start giving money from your IRA to a charity, tax-free. Remember that when you take out money from your IRA to spend it yourself, you have to pay the tax due on it. But in this instance, if the money gets sent directly to a charity, you can avoid the tax.

For our clients who are charitably minded, we use this strategy instead of having them give to charities out of pocket. When they contribute through their IRA, they can save a significant amount of taxes over time.

But what if you're not seventy and a half yet? Do you still need to know about this right now? The answer is yes. Knowing about the QCD now is a good reason why you wouldn't convert as much money over to the Roth IRA as you thought you might. You'll have enough money in tax-deferred accounts to give to charities over time.

Here's how that could look. Let's say you give $10,000 to your favorite charity every year, and you expect to do that going into retirement. In that case, you would probably want to leave at least $200,000 in the tax-deferred account that can be portioned off for this purpose during your retirement. There's no need to convert it and pay a tax if you plan to give it to the charity and would pay no tax anyway.

I mentioned the donor-advised fund (DAF) strategy earlier. We use that strategy until the age of seventy and a half, before the QCDs can begin. Once you reach the age of seventy-three or seventy-five, you can start giving a portion or all of your RMDs to a charity, and you won't have to take out as much from your RMD that gets counted as income. As you can see, this is another reason for not converting all your tax-deferred-bucket funds into a Roth.

Let's now discuss a few more of the advanced options that could be used in the tax-free bucket.

Life Insurance

Insurance? Tax-free? Well, some would argue that life insurance can be considered part of the tax-free bucket, which is why I mention it here. I'm not always the biggest fan of tax-free income from life insurance. For those in or near retirement, the cost of insurance can be high, so this strategy may not be as advantageous. I'm not telling you not to do it. I'm telling you to be aware and beware as you determine if it makes sense for you.

That said, Midwestern Millionaires could use life insurance when it comes to legacy planning, and the tax-free element is a benefit in that case. If you leave life insurance to a beneficiary, the death benefit amount is tax-free. For example, let's say you put $100,000 into a life insurance policy, and now the death benefit is worth $300,000. When you pass, your beneficiary pays no tax on the $300,000. This means any growth above the amount you put in is tax-free. This can add extra value to your beneficiaries. Especially if you expect them to be in a higher tax bracket or expect tax rates to be higher when you pass away.

Long-term care coverage is another big concern for many retirees nowadays. People are living longer but not necessarily healthier, and American healthcare of all kinds is costly and gets more expensive year after year. By subscribing to an appropriate life insurance policy with a feature that allows you to access the death benefit while you're living *and* to use the funds for long-term healthcare needs, these withdrawals would be tax-free to you. This allows you to use the life insurance policy for more than the traditional death benefit amount going to a beneficiary when you pass away.

This is yet another reason why you will benefit from comprehensive tax planning; it affects your healthcare planning for your later years.

The other tax-free benefit of life insurance is that the residual death benefit values left to heirs are free from estate tax.

But remember life insurance isn't for everyone. You must be healthy enough to be insurable, but deciding to choose life insurance also depends on your goals and situation. Not all our Midwestern Millionaire clients use life insurance. It is one tool in the large toolbox that can make sense for some.

Asset Location and Taxes

One thing we like to see is asset location, where you strategically and specifically invest assets in each of these buckets. For example, if we have a Roth IRA, we want to put our more growth-oriented investments in our tax-free bucket and then that large amount of growth is tax-free as it continues to compound.

What about the money you want to hold more safely? You may want to consider more conservative investments. Many of the people we work with who are in or near retirement and are Midwestern Millionaires want to take some chips off the table at this point in their lives. They've taken enough risk over the years. Their money has grown. They don't need to continue to seek 50 percent returns every year. Quite the contrary. Now they need consistent, predictable, and reliable returns so that a portion of their retirement savings is protected to produce income or to be there if or when they need it.

Maybe the best place for this investment would be in the tax-deferred bucket. This would be where your IRA is, and the idea is that protected investments may not grow so quickly, and we don't have to worry about paying as much tax on the growth in the future. This may also be the place we want to take income from now, if needed, while tax rates are lower.

We also want to have more tax-efficient investments in the taxable bucket. We don't want to invest in mutual funds and worry about "phantom gains." This is where gains are realized every year, increasing our income, and we're not able to plan to reduce those capital gains over time. We advise clients to invest in individual stocks or exchange-traded funds (ETFs) that don't have a lot of turnover. That allows us to control the capital gains and make trades and changes when desired, versus letting an anonymous investment fund manager decide for us. An investment fund manager does not understand your complete financial plan; we do.

Being more tax efficient will give you more control to do what you want when you want and hopefully give you more return over time because of tax-smart investing strategies. Also, as we've already discussed, we may want to be careful in being conservative. These funds as protected options tend to cause taxes to be less preferential (ordinary income tax rates versus capital gains). If you can hold the amount you want protected in your IRA and keep your taxable money on the growth side of your plan, then that may make more sense and provide more tax alpha to your returns. (Think of tax alpha as the ability to save money on taxes, which leads you to having more money and providing higher after-tax returns on your investments.)

The Tax Buckets in Summary

The last thing I'll mention about the three buckets is to be careful about how you invest your money into each one. We don't want you to have all your money in only one of these buckets. We look for a balance. We call this "tax diversification."

As a younger earner, you may have focused on, say, maxing out the 401(k) your employer offered. Later, though, you may want to diversify and fund the other buckets. You've probably heard that saying about not putting all your eggs in one basket. Do you have all your money in Bitcoin? Probably not. You probably follow a diversified approach with your investments, and that's what you may want to consider when it comes to these three tax buckets.

As I stated earlier, right now most Americans have most of their money in the tax-deferred bucket. We would want to look for ways to shift some of that over to the tax-free bucket. For those with more funds in the taxable bucket, we would also look for ways to shift that into a tax-free bucket.

We don't want everything in the tax-free bucket because there are advantages of having money in the tax-deferred or taxable buckets. And don't forget that we have to make good use of the standard deduction every year. You may also look at the advantages of gifting to charities through QCDs. We don't want to leave any tax-free money on the table.

7

SOCIAL SECURITY STRATEGIES

Everyone understands the general rules of Social Security:

- You can choose when to begin your Social Security benefits, and you can collect them early (age sixty-two) if you're willing to take a lesser amount for life.

- Taking your benefit at the "full" age (age sixty-six or sixty-seven) pays you 100 percent of your earned benefits—for life.

- Waiting until age seventy increases the amount to its maximum—for life.

The Social Security benefit is the United States' equivalent of a "guaranteed lifetime income." Once you start your benefit payments, the amount is guaranteed to you for life (with some upward cost-of-living adjustments along the way).

A Midwestern Millionaire, however, also wants to understand the tax picture. And believe it or not, tax is an issue with Social Security, too, unless you plan ahead.

Social Security Tax Torpedo

I've mentioned the Social Security tax torpedo and feel I need to explain it in depth. Many people aren't aware of what it is and how much it costs them.

The Social Security tax torpedo occurs when, due to your higher overall income, 85 percent of your Social Security benefit could now be taxable at the federal level as income. Some retirees may also face state-level taxation on their Social Security benefits, as nine states still tax Social Security income as of 2024.[11]

The taxation of Social Security benefits is based on a complex formula called provisional income, which considers half of your Social Security benefit, pensions, wages, and investment income. Adding those up gives you your

---

11   Katelyn Washington, "Will Retirees Stop Paying Tax on Social Security Next Year?" updated February 11, 2024, accessed July 2024, https://www.kiplinger.com/taxes/will-tax-on-social-security-benefits-be-eliminated.

provisional income, which is taken to the following chart to determine how much of it is taxable.

Taxation of Social Security Benefits		
Filing Status	Provisional Income	Social Security subject to Tax
Married Filing Jointly	Under $32,000	0
	$32,000 - $44,000	Up to 50%
	Over $44,000	Up to 85%
Single	Under $25,000	0
	$25,000 - $34,000	Up to 50%
	Over $34,000	Up to 85%

Source: "Income Taxes and Your Social Security Benefit," Social Security Administration, https://www-origin.ssa.gov/benefits/retirement/planner/taxes.html

Your benefit could be tax-free to you, and it is tax-free for people who don't have as much income in retirement. In the chart above, you will see Social Security is not taxed for the married couple filing jointly with a provisional income under $32,000, or for the single filer with a provisional income under $25,000.

In other words, Social Security benefits are tax-free for individuals with low total or provisional income levels. But that's not our Midwestern Millionaire, is it? It's probably not you either.

Like many Midwestern Millionaires earning more in retirement, you may find that 85 percent of your Social Security is taxable, as shown in that same chart. If you don't plan the right way, your RMDs alone could put you there. Although, if we can start reducing those RMDs now, before the age of seventy-three or seventy-five, then you may have the opportunity to get your Social Security either tax-free or less taxable. Note: Many of the people we work with have pensions. It is a niche of ours as only 20 percent of people have them nowadays,[12] which means their pension income in retirement may not allow them to get Social Security tax-free or less taxable. The following example is for those without a pension. Also, those with a pension may face WEP or GPO and may get little to no Social Security Benefit. If you have a pension and are a Midwestern Millionaire, it is even more important to get expert help from a specialist who knows the ins and outs of pension planning.

I agree it's a complex calculation to determine how much Social Security tax you have to pay since it's based on your provisional income, but the following chart takes those calculations and makes it easily visible.

---

[12] "New AARP Survey: 1 in 5 Americans Ages 50+ Have No Retirement Savings and Over Half Worry They Will Not Have Enough to Last in Retirement," AARP, April 24, 2024, https://press.aarp.org/2024-4-24-New-AARP-Survey-1-in-5-Americans-Ages-50-Have-No-Retirement-Savings.

SOCIAL SECURITY STRATEGIES

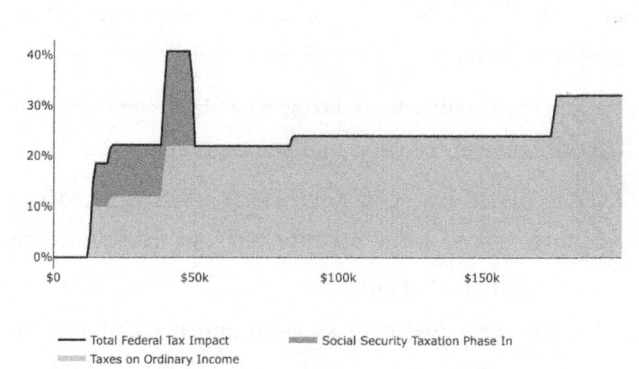

Tax Impact of the Next $1,000.00 in Ordinary Income

— Total Federal Tax Impact   ▬▬ Social Security Taxation Phase In
▬▬ Taxes on Ordinary Income

Source: Joe F. Schmitz Jr., CFP®, ChFC®, CKA®, "Will You Pay Higher Taxes in Retirement?" Kiplinger.com, May 10, 2023, https://www.kiplinger.com/retirement/will-you-pay-higher-taxes-in-retirement.

The chart shows the impact of taking money from your investments in retirement. The vertical bar is the tax bracket, and the horizontal bar is your income. It shows at which point your Social Security will start to become taxable, and in which tax bracket, after your standard deduction.

Moving to the right, along the horizontal bar, you will see that as soon as you start to take out more money from your tax-deferred investments, you start to force more of your Social Security to become taxable. If you take out just under $20,000 from your tax-deferred investments, you'll use not only the standard deduction but also the early part of the provisional income amount that calculates the taxation of Social Security to allow that $20,000 withdrawal to still be tax-free.

If you take out $80,000 from your tax-deferred investments, you'll force Social Security to become nearly fully taxable (85 percent).

You're probably wondering what that steep peak is all about between $60,000 and $80,000. That's the Social Security tax torpedo. This is where you could pay a 40 percent tax by forcing your Social Security and your federal income tax bracket into higher amounts.

If you were just over $60,000 and decided to take $10,000 from a tax-deferred account to increase your income that year, you could force yourself to pay $4,000 of taxes and get to keep only $6,000.

This can be a rough place to be. That's why it's important for the Midwestern Millionaire who wants to keep as much of their hard-earned money as they can to know how investment withdrawals affect the tax picture in retirement.

We like to run these numbers for our clients every year to make sure they're not paying more taxes than they need to. For most of our clients, we like to see them before that Social Security tax torpedo—or in the 0 percent tax bracket. It isn't always reasonable for everyone to be there, but for those we can get there, they can save some money and taxes over time.

I'll talk further about how to be in a low-income situation to use the 0 percent bracket in retirement. I probably scared you when I said you have to live retirement with a lower income, but I'm not telling you to eat ramen noodles every day—far from it! What I am telling you is if you can do proactive tax and income planning before you get to retirement, the IRS could consider you low income while still living on, for example, $100,000 a year.

How does that look? We have a couple living on $100,000 a year who banks their Social Security tax-free. They're Midwestern Millionaires, just like you. They've saved over $1 million. They're living what I call "a tax-free retirement." It could be a realistic opportunity for you.

Organizing your finances the right way can allow you to spend more money in retirement and leave more of a legacy. So let's discuss what this looks like.

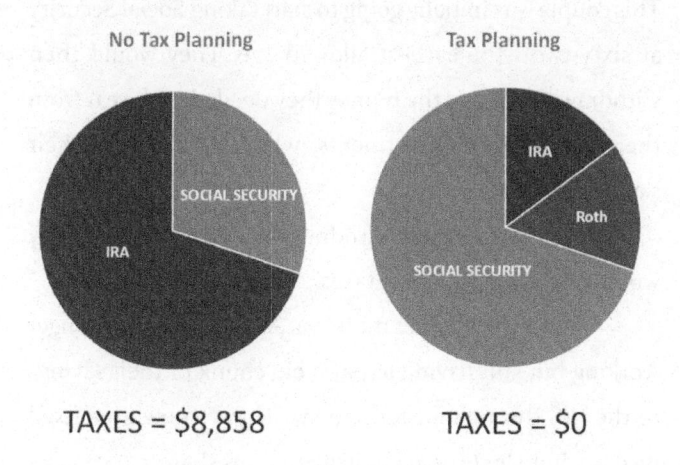

No Tax Planning

IRA / SOCIAL SECURITY

TAXES = $8,858

Tax Planning

IRA / Roth / SOCIAL SECURITY

TAXES = $0

I often use the preceding chart to illustrate the impact of tax-efficient income planning and retirement. This illustration is meant to give you a high-level understanding of how all this works together. This is by no means a recommendation of how you should plan, since everyone's situation is different. It's important to seek professional guidance on your specific situation.

The chart above is a real-life example with the real numbers of one of our clients we've been able to help over time who needed $100,000 of income per year. You'll also see how you could potentially get your Social Security tax-free by planning a specific way.

In the chart, we have Option A: No Tax Planning. Option A would be to not do any planning and withdraw what you need, doing what Uncle Sam said to do, tax-wise. This couple was initially going to start taking Social Security at sixty-two—the earliest allowed age. They would then withdraw the rest of the money they needed each year from their tax-deferred investments, which is where all their savings were.

In managing their withdrawals in this manner, they would be paying $8,858 in taxes.

What always strikes me is that Americans are no longer working but still having to pay a big chunk of their savings to the IRS throughout retirement. They're now on a fixed income, but Uncle Sam is still getting his share.

But is it Uncle Sam's fair share?

This is the no-planning approach far too many Americans adopt. It's where you have no control, and you could end up paying more in taxes if tax rates go up. Remember, a Midwestern Millionaire's concern is to protect what they have and to keep as much of their hard-earned money as legitimately possible.

It's not how much you take out of your accounts in retirement. It's how much of it you keep. In this example, the couple could only keep $91,142. They needed $100,000 to live on. That created a gap, right? If they decided to do things differently and get a plan in place, what would that look like?

The second approach is Option B: Tax Planning. We analyze the whole financial picture, then implement tax-saving strategies to pay no tax in the future. Option B is where we can implement a plan over time with some of the strategies we've discussed—but we need to review each client's full financial picture to know which specific strategies are optimal.

We might decide that it makes sense to wait until age seventy to take Social Security—when your benefit reaches and stays at its highest amount. This isn't always what we recommend; when to take Social Security depends on many factors.

This couple waited until age seventy to do some tax planning and convert some of their tax-deferred dollars to

Roth at lower tax rates. They didn't immediately need or take the extra income from Social Security. This also allowed them to spend down some of their tax-deferred investments while they waited for their Social Security benefit to grow over time. Because both of them waited until age seventy, they were able to accumulate nearly double the amount in their Social Security and be more tax efficient.

Since they were able to diversify their tax portfolio and have some balance of Roth, they now had control out of which bucket to withdraw money. They could now create their income exactly how they wanted.

What we can learn from the tax planning example:

- If we take money from the Roth, how much tax do we pay? Zero dollars.

- If we're able to keep our Social Security provisional income under the taxable limits, how much of our Social Security is taxable? Zero dollars.

- If we take money from the tax-deferred account under the standard deduction, how much tax do we pay? Zero dollars.

This is how you live a tax-free retirement.

Now understand that this illustration isn't all sunshine and rainbows. To get money into the Roth, this client did have to pay taxes up front. When we ran the numbers for this client's situation, however, it made sense to pay the taxes early. Why? It led to much more lifetime tax savings than what they had to pay up front. For them, it led to over $100,000 of projected tax savings over their lifetime and increased their projected net worth at the end of time.

I always want to emphasize the importance of doing your research, getting professional advice, and having a professional team run your numbers. Many firms don't do this level of planning. If you're working with a financial planning team who specializes in tax planning and talks to you about everything we've mentioned so far, then I'm sure they're doing this for you to ensure you're getting the income you need in retirement the right way.

I'm also sure they've started to prepare in advance so you can get ahead of tax planning and income planning to have these different options. If that's the case, then you have a great team, and I congratulate you. We don't see it often. We usually hear far too many people say, "My financial advisor never talks about tax planning and how it works into the rest of my financial plan."

If you're working with a financial planner who doesn't do this planning, then you may have missed some opportunities, and you may want to seek an expert who can help with more advanced planning. But don't worry. As I always say, you can't change the past, but you can change the future. The key is to take action now.

8

MEDICARE PREMIUM STRATEGIES

What is this Medicare program? In a nutshell, Medicare is a federal health insurance program. It's primarily for people aged sixty-five and older, but it offers benefits for some younger individuals with specific disabilities or conditions.

Medicare consists of different parts covering various aspects of healthcare, including hospital insurance (Part A), medical insurance (Part B), Medicare Advantage plans (Part C), and prescription drug coverage (Part D).[13] In its basic form of Parts A, B, and D, the program is known as traditional Medicare.

---

13   "Parts of Medicare," Medicare.gov, https://www.medicare.gov/basics/get-started-with-medicare/medicare-basics/parts-of-medicare; Julie Kagan, "What Is Medicare? How It Works, Who Qualifies, and How to Enroll," updated September 20, 2024, https://www.investopedia.com/terms/m/medicare.asp.

There is a premium attached to Medicare, like all insurance coverage. It's payable on an individual (not family) basis. But how much is that premium? Similar to the tax code that's written in pencil, the answer here is "it depends."

Uncle Sam and Aunt IRMAA

If Uncle Sam rules the tax code, Aunt IRMAA runs the Medicare premium calculations for us. As I defined earlier, IRMAA stands for "income-related monthly adjustment amount," which is the insurance premium that those who opt into Medicare Part B and Part D pay in addition to their standard Medicare premium.

Aunt IRMAA, like Uncle Sam, is a big concern for the Midwestern Millionaire.

Those who aren't Midwestern Millionaires may have never heard of this "aunt" and may not have planned for it (or need to).

This is a concern for those who will have a higher income in the two years before age sixty-five. The unfortunate news about this Medicare IRMAA—besides the fact that no one tells you about it until it's usually too late to plan—is you could end up paying more for healthcare throughout your retirement while not getting better benefits and coverage. Study the following chart, and you'll understand how this works. In short, the higher your income, the higher your Medicare premiums.

Remember, conscientious earners, diligent savers, and Midwestern Millionaires are being penalized for doing the right thing over the years. You must plan strategically if you're going to turn the rules in your favor. This can be done through proper income and tax planning as discussed throughout this book.

Medicare Premiums		
If your yearly income in 2023 was:		You pay each month in 2025:
File individual tax return	File joint tax return	
$106,000 or less	$212,000 or less	$185.00
above $106,000 up to $133,000	above $212,000 up to $266,000	$259.00
above $133,000 up to $167,000	above $266,000 up to $334,000	$370.00
above $167,000 up to $200,000	above $334,000 up to $400,000	$480.90
above $200,000 less than $500,000	above $400,000 less than $750,000	$591.90
$500,000 or above	$750,000 or above	$628.90

Source: "2025 Medicare Parts A & B Premiums and Deductibles," Centers for Medicare and Medicaid Services, November 8, 2024, https://www.cms.gov/newsroom/fact-sheets/2025-medicare-parts-b-premiums-and-deductibles.

The previous chart outlines the brackets that determine how much your Medicare will cost. Note that this goes back two years. If your income for this calculation was $300,000 at age sixty-three, then you would be in the fourth tier and be required to pay $480.90 a month instead of the base tier of $185.00. That's a lot of extra money for the same coverage.

If you're in this position, the good news is you could potentially file an appeal based on a life-changing event to get this cost reduced to the first tier. We do this often with our clients and have much success.

The other thing to keep in mind with Medicare premiums is Roth conversions. If you're sixty-three or older and doing Roth conversions, you need to start paying attention to your Medicare premiums. You shouldn't be discouraged from doing Roth conversions, but you need to be extremely focused, because if you're even one dollar over the limit, you'll pay an increased premium. For many of our clients, the question becomes this: Does paying more for Medicare for one year lead us to paying less for Medicare in subsequent years? We don't always advocate paying more in Medicare premiums to do Roth conversions, but it makes sense for some people. It depends on your specific situation. You should never rely on cookie-cutter advice when it comes to your life savings.

ESTATE PLANNING AND TRANSFERRING WEALTH

We will now talk about something extremely important, yet something people don't like to think about. It's estate planning, or what I call "planning for the end of life."

Estate planning is the process of organizing and managing your wealth—your physical assets and money—so that upon your death, your wealth will do three things:

- Pass to the beneficiaries you choose

- Pass in a legally recognized, indisputable manner

- Transmit in a tax-efficient manner for you and the beneficiaries.

You've probably heard estate planning is something everyone should do, and I agree with that. How to do it is the confusing part, and because of this, only 33 percent of Americans die with an estate plan in place.[14]

The Midwestern Millionaire takes this aspect of planning very seriously. Remember: The more assets you have, the more you have to protect and thus the more advanced planning that will be required.

Protecting the spouse is often the number one goal in estate planning for those we work with, in addition to avoiding probate and passing on as much wealth as possible to loved ones. This can be known as "generational planning." It's extremely important to me, and it's why I started and built my firm the way I have. Clients often tell us this is one of the things they love most about working with us. They know we will be there not only for their retirement but also for their kids and grandkids.

I saw this firsthand with my mentor, the woman I mentioned in chapter 5, who got me into the financial planning industry. Seeing her serve three generations of her family showed me how our influence can last for generations to come if we can help these families do the right thing and transfer their wealth appropriately. With the average advisor

---

14 "Estate Planning Statistics to Read Before Writing Your Will," LegalZoom, updated July 30, 2024, accessed September 10, 2024, https://www.legalzoom.com/articles/estate-planning-statistics.

in our industry being fifty-six years of age,[15] this is something not all advisors can say.

The Midwestern Millionaire understands that estate document creation isn't DIY planning. They need a trained attorney practicing in estates and trusts. The attorney should work alongside your tax expert and your financial planner to ensure nothing is missing. We also believe these professionals should be in the same location so they can collaborate and be in meetings together when crafting plans.

When it comes to the legal documents that are part of estate planning, we often consider the following for our clients:

- A healthcare power of attorney

- A financial power of attorney

- A last will and testament

- A living will

- One or more trusts

---

15   "Time-Starved US Financial Advisors Considering Alternative Options, J.D. Power Finds," J.D. Power, July 5, 2023, accessed September 10, 2024, https://www.jdpower.com/business/press-releases/2023-us-financial-advisor-satisfaction-study.

Taken together, the documents ensure that all decisions will be made smoothly and according to the client's expressed wishes at their passing or if they become disabled or incapacitated. Now, estate planning documents are important, but for the Midwestern Millionaire, they're only a small piece of the estate planning picture. We'll discuss the other important considerations to have in place when it comes to this topic.

Do You Need a Trust?

We're often asked, "Do I need a trust?" To answer it concisely, not all our clients need a trust. One reason we have our clients work closely with an estate planning attorney is to establish whether a trust would be a useful planning tool. If yes, the attorney prepares the documents they need. And then you will want to make sure you get the right trust at the right price.

As a general guideline, those with more complex financial or family situations may want to consider creating one or more trusts.

The complexity I'm speaking of might involve the following:

- You want to be more diligent and intentional about how your money is transferred when you pass

- You own multiple properties in one or more states

- You own one or more businesses or have partnerships in business

- You have minor children to care for

- You have a child with a lifetime handicap or disability that requires special care (and funding for it)

- You have express wishes on how you want to be cared for if you're in poor health near the end of your days

- You have adult children you can't trust to be wise with money or assets

- You have kids who don't need help at this time, and you would rather see multigenerational wealth built over time in your family's name

- You want your wealth to skip one generation of heirs—bypassing your kids—but go to your grandkids instead

- You have children from more than one marriage or relationship who may or may not lay claim to a portion of your wealth upon your death

- You want protections to keep your money in your bloodline

- You want to prevent wealth from being passed to a divorced spouse or the children of that prior union

- You want to reduce or avoid estate taxes

- You have any other combination of wishes

Most people think you need a trust to avoid probate. It's true that trusts can help avoid probate; however, in some states you may not need a trust to ensure all your assets pass to your loved ones while still avoiding probate. This is where I caution you to consult professionals who know your state laws.

For example, let's say you live in Ohio, where our home office is. All you have is an IRA, your house, and your bank accounts. As long as you've listed a beneficiary on your IRA, designated a "transfer on death" on your house, and designated a "payable on death" on your bank accounts, none of your assets will go to probate. In other words, don't pay the extra money to get a trust if none of the points above apply to you.

We work with clients all across the country, and some states don't allow you to pass your house via a transfer on death designation to avoid probate. In these instances, it could make more sense to get a trust. Another point on trusts—and to bring this full circle to the basics—is that most trusts don't get funded once they're created. All the documents get put into a nice professional binder, but nothing happens after that. If you pass away, that trust would do nothing for your estate or heirs.

One more step is required.

You must fund the trusts. In other words, you must assign the trust to the accounts you have and be sure they are funded. This step sounds obvious, but many law firms won't do this for you and will require you to get this done on your own. Again, this is why we recommend working with an estate planning team that collaborates with your financial planning team, or else things can get missed and cause more work. Remember, you're a Midwestern Millionaire who requires a different plan and team than most of your peers.

Before we continue discussing trusts, let's take a step back and talk about why other types of trusts could be beneficial. Let's get some clarity about estate taxes.

What Are Estate Taxes?

Estate tax is a tax that can be assessed on your assets when you pass. Recently and currently, estate tax has been less of a planning item as the asset value limit has been so high. Although the estate tax was much lower in the past, it is subject to change. Remember that the tax codes—and therefore the tax rates—are written in pencil.

From the following chart, we see a "lifetime exemption," which means any amount of your net worth under this amount is not subject to the estate tax. Thus, for an individual who passed in 2002, their estate could have faced up to a 50 percent tax rate for its value over $1 million. If they had $3 million at that time, then the estate would have paid up to $1 million in estate taxes (50 percent tax on $2 million).

Going all the way back to 1997 (not shown on this chart), the estate value limit or exemption was $600,000 and that estate tax rate was 55 percent. Any estate value over $600,000 would have been taxed at 55 percent. In 2025, as I write this, the estate exemption amount is $13,990,000. Thus, any estate value above that amount is taxable at a 40 percent rate.

The federal estate tax isn't the only tax due in these instances. The estate tax rate is in addition to any federal taxes and state taxes your beneficiaries would also pay.

So here's an interesting question: Given the recent history of rates from 35 to 50 percent and value ceilings from $600,000 to $13,990,000, could any of these numbers come back? In other words, could the authorities lower the estate lifetime exemption limit *and* increase the estate tax rate?

You're shrugging and saying, "Of course, they could."

Such a scenario would mean that estate tax would affect more families who today would say, "We don't have nearly enough assets to be concerned." If you're saying such a thing, then I may agree with you...today. Although if you're a true Midwestern Millionaire, then your net worth is at least $1 million or more and likely growing. Our advice is to be aware of this limit.

Do you see how, over time, the authorities have already proven they can use their pencils and erasers to write this part of the tax code? Why wouldn't they do it again? No one knows for certain what that tax code pencil will be doing in the future, but based on the facts I have access to, I would be shocked if the estate lifetime exemption limits don't start to come down.

US Estate and Gift Tax Exemptions and Tax Rates

Year	Lifetime Exemption	Tax Rates
2001	$675,000	55 percent
2002	$1 million	50 percent
2003	$1 million	49 percent
2004	$1.5 million	48 percent
2005	$1.5 million	47 percent
2006	$2 million	46 percent
2007	$2 million	45 percent
2008	$2 million	45 percent
2009	$3.5 million	45 percent
2010	Repealed	0 percent
2011	$5 million	35 percent
2012	$5.12 million	35 percent
2013	$5.25 million	40 percent
2014	$5.34 million	40 percent
2015	$5.43 million	40 percent
2016	$5.45 million	40 percent
2017	$5.49 million	40 percent
2018	$11.18 million	40 percent
2019	$11.4 million	40 percent
2020	$11.58 million	40 percent
2021	$11.7 million	40 percent
2022	$12.06 million	40 percent
2023	$12.92 million	40 percent
2024	$13.61 million	40 percent

In our office, we have an estate tax calculator we use with our clients to see if estate taxes are something we need to start planning for. We first start by understanding our clients' goals and their financial and family circumstances. Then we calculate how big of a concern this could be. We finally discuss, choose, and layer in strategies that would lower the potential estate tax they may have to pay.

Let's walk through some of the more popular strategies we haven't mentioned yet that could be useful here. We'll look at trusts, gifting, and giving, as well as how to avoid a couple of devastating penalties many Americans don't even know about.

Irrevocable Trusts

Let me get back to trusts here and discuss Midwestern Millionaires who may need a trust to protect them from estate taxes. Putting assets in an irrevocable trust means you would lose access to the assets you put in this kind of trust. The idea is to move assets out of your estate so they can't be counted as part of your estate's value for estate tax purposes when you pass away.

Many people get concerned about that, and if that's you, then this certainly may not be an option for you. This is for those trying to protect their assets and giving up control of a small portion of their assets (we don't give up control of everything, obviously) to pass more of their wealth to their loved ones. We would only recommend this if we knew for certain (as certain as we can be, at least, since anything can happen at any time) that they won't use all their assets or a specific asset.

Not everyone will need an irrevocable trust today with the high estate-tax limits we have, but this is something that must be on their radar. You know the authorities are almost always trying to find ways to further tax the wealthy to get more federal tax revenue.

Another way you could use this kind of irrevocable trust is to do what's called generation skipping. You wouldn't give the money to your children but instead give it to the grandkids. This could be used if you know your kids will not need the wealth, and you want the next generations to be well taken care of.

You may not avoid estate taxes altogether when you employ this strategy. This issue will still be something the grandkids will likely have to face and plan for. The assets could be subject to estate taxes due to the growth of the assets over time, but it could allow you to kick the can down the road and maybe not have to worry about it for another fifty-plus years. That buys the coming generation a lot of time to do additional planning and discover strategies to reduce their own tax burden.

This strategy will also allow your kids to not have to worry about it and save money on legal fees in getting additional trusts and planning set up.

Irrevocable Life Insurance Trust

I want to share one more trust that Midwestern Millionaires could use to lessen the estate tax issue and benefit from its multiple layers of benefits. This trust (another "irrevocable" one) is called an irrevocable life insurance trust (ILIT), and it can be used for life insurance.

You might ask, "Why would I need life insurance at this point? I may have needed it during my earning years and when I was raising children, but now that I have accumulated enough wealth, I'm self-insured." And you would most likely be correct about that. This isn't a strategy to ensure your spouse has enough money after you pass.

The ILIT is used to ensure your loved ones get as much wealth passed to them in the most tax-efficient way possible. It is this tax efficiency that makes the ILIT an advantage as life insurance for the Midwestern Millionaire.

We already talked about the many tax-free benefits of life insurance earlier in the book, but now I want to focus on the estate tax benefits.

Free from Estate Tax

To be free from estate taxes, you would need to set up the ILIT as we discussed earlier. When you put your life insurance policy in an ILIT, it's out of your estate (as the term "irrevocable" suggests) and would not be subject to estate taxes.

If you don't do an ILIT, and you find your assets push you past the estate tax exemption limit, then you'll be forced to pay estate taxes on that policy. Not federal taxes but estate taxes. An ILIT can allow you to say no to both of those taxes. This is especially smart if your primary goal is to leave the life insurance to your beneficiary, and you don't plan to access its cash value for any purpose. You might as well get it out of your estate, or at least that's the idea here.

Not every strategy makes sense for every Midwestern Millionaire, so do the research or work with a professional team to see if this makes sense for you. It may not be needed for as simple a reason as you're not looking to leave behind money for your loved ones. If so, then get busy spending, if that's you. Or find a charity you're passionate about. You can't take this money with you.

Additional Protection for You and Your Family: Personal Liability Umbrella Policy

Considering that our Midwestern Millionaires have more assets than many people, they also have more at risk. We almost always recommend our clients with millions of dollars of net worth get a personal liability umbrella policy (PLUP).

What is a PLUP? It's a policy designed to provide an extra layer of financial protection for your assets and future earnings in case of major lawsuits or claims that exceed your standard insurance coverage limits. In other words, you're covered in case you get sued in a way that goes above and beyond your home and auto insurance coverage.

The PLUP is an easy decision to have when you're a high-net-worth individual. You can be sued for the oddest reasons. We had a client who was walking his dog, and it bit someone. Sure enough, the person that was bitten sued our client. But our client had a PLUP that covered the event. They weren't dramatically affected financially.

As you know, we're a litigious culture, and it's up to you to protect yourself. The cost is only hundreds of dollars a year to protect millions. It's well worth it.

Spousal Planning and the Widow(er)'s Penalty

Spousal planning is another big concern of Midwestern Millionaires. They want their spouse to be taken care of after they pass. There are three issues we must plan for here.

1. The Consolidation and Centralization of the Plans

The goal is that the spouse doesn't have to worry about organizing the estate when they're grieving. Organizing the estate—knowing who the advisor team is, what has been arranged, where the paperwork is located—can be made easy when the right estate planning has been undertaken.

Grieving for the loss of a loved one is no easy task. It's surely better when you can put all your energy and focus toward overcoming the loss instead of putting focus on your financial plan.

2. The Tax Issues for the Surviving Spouse

When one spouse passes, the tax brackets will now move from married filing jointly to single. This could force the surviving spouse to pay nearly double the amount in taxes since their standard deduction gets cut in half and their tax brackets get cut in half.

3. The Changes in Social Security

When one spouse passes, the surviving spouse loses one of the two Social Security benefits. They get to keep the higher of the two, but the other one goes away. This could be a significant loss of income.

These last two concerns—taxation and Social Security loss—are called the widow(er)'s penalty. For many of our clients who lose a spouse, they can easily end up with $30,000–$40,000 less in income, if not more, because of losing one of the Social Security benefits and the increased taxes.

The good news is if you proactively tax plan now while you and your spouse are living, you can use the married filing jointly tax brackets and other strategies to best position your spouse if something were to happen.

The Kiddo's Penalty

The next tax planning consideration is what can be referred to as the kiddo's penalty. This is a potential penalty to your children when they are the beneficiary of your IRA.

New rules state that funds in an IRA passed to your children must be withdrawn over ten years. This could be a recipe for tax disaster for your children, if they earn good money are in a higher tax bracket, and if you've saved a significant amount in your IRA. Your children may have to pay significant taxes, which ultimately means less of your wealth gets passed down to them.

Let's say you have $2 million in your IRA, and you have two children who will inherit this wealth. They will each get $1 million and be required to take it out over ten years. That could be an average of $100,000 a year (plus growth), which would be on top of the income they're currently making at unknown tax rates in the future.

We talked about the power of the Roth and that could be an opportunity for those looking to plan for this and leave more to their kids and less to Uncle Sam. The Roth still forces your children to take the money out over ten years, but now they won't have to count it toward income. Their taxable income won't be higher since a Roth is tax-free when withdrawn.

Gifting and Giving

If you find yourself giving to charities—or wishing to give your children money during your lifetime—then you can most likely benefit from one or more tax-planning strategies to save some money. Gifting now to your kids is an estate-planning strategy the wealthy have always used, and it's something we often do with clients.

The government gives you a certain limit you can give/gift each year while having it not count toward your estate tax limit. For 2025, that limit is $19,000. This means $19,000 could be given per spouse per child per year with no tax burden.

Gifting can be used in addition to a trust or as a stand-alone strategy. It can include giving to your loved ones now as well as giving to charities now or in the future. The amount of wealth you could remove from your estate over time could therefore be substantial. Gifting also allows your loved ones to benefit from the wealth you have now when they might need it most, whether it helps them save for retirement, or it gets spent on items they need now.

The giving can involve children or charities. Since we don't have to worry about giving as much money to Uncle Sam with all the proactive tax-smart planning and staying on top of other risks that could take your money, we can now focus on the bigger picture of who will enjoy the wealth you have worked hard for.

When it comes to giving to your children, I always preface this conversation by asking how much is enough for the children. I never discourage someone from giving to their children. This is your money, and you need to decide what you want to do. Obviously, we see situations where millions of dollars are left to the kids, and they do the right thing. You may have heard that most inheritances are spent right away, and that's true. Oftentimes, the inheritance you provided is spent in a way that you would have never spent it nor would have approved of.

That's why we feel it is important to have a conversation with your children to share what your purpose and values are with this money and how you would like to see them use it. But it's all talk, talk, talk. They will still spend the money the way they want when you're gone. If this is an important issue for you, you could set up a trust that will specify how it is paid out and how it is used.

We also recommend family meetings where you sit down with your children to share these purposes and values with them and to ensure they know what to expect. Sometimes children can be surprised at the large nest egg that's being left to them. Or they might be dismayed because they thought there would be much more, and they were planning for that larger sum. These family meetings are something we do for our clients; we help facilitate them and ensure they go well.

The key is to get your children or family members to understand there could be nothing left at all, but if there is, you have a plan for what to expect. This allows them to be best set up for success. With the families we serve, we always like to work with not only them but also their children. This allows us to ensure the smooth transfer of generational wealth. It allows us to make it easy for the children when they do inherit that money and to also ensure that the values and mission are lived out.

The sooner we can start working with the children, the better, as we can start building habits and a complex financial plan from the beginning. Then the inheritance is the icing on the cake that allows them to meet their goals.

A Multidisciplinary Team: Consolidation and Collaboration

Midwestern Millionaires like to know they're working with a multidisciplinary team, preferably working together under one roof. They want all kinds of specialists to help them not miss anything. They want to make sure their estate planning attorney, certified public accountant (CPA), and CERTIFIED FINANCIAL PLANNER® are collaborating and working together on their behalf and in their best interests.

The Midwestern Millionaire's planning, calculations, and strategies can't all be done by one person. That's our take. Our firm involves the following professionals in addition to all of our financial planners:

- **Attorney.** We coordinate with the estate planning attorney and have an elder law attorney who meets with our clients at our office or virtually.

- **Certified public accountant.** We have in-house CPAs who do the tax preparation and complete our clients' tax returns, while also ensuring that the comprehensive tax planning our advisor team does gets implemented on the tax return the right way.

- **Medicare expert.** We have a trained Medicare expert who will get our clients the optimal coverage when they reach age sixty-five or retire so they don't have to worry about shopping around for the right coverage.

- **Insurance professional.** We help our clients get the right health insurance coverage in place (in advance of or additional to traditional Medicare) if they retire before age sixty-five, and we help them with any other insurance needs like life insurance.

Midwestern Millionaires want to know they're maximizing their hard-earned assets and not leaving money on the table—not having money left unprotected from unnecessary taxation. This also means they don't want accounts at multiple different institutions. They prefer to consolidate. They want all their assets with one team at one custodian (the place holding your investable assets).

They may not want all their eggs in one basket when it comes to the type of investments they have at one custodian, but they do want all their assets in one place so they get one statement each month. Another added advantage is that their beneficiaries don't have the burden of trying to determine where everything is after they've passed.

When you have accumulated as much as the Midwestern Millionaire, consolidation and a multidisciplinary team that collaborates become even more important the more assets you accumulate to get everything working together and in harmony.

10
THE PURPOSE OF MONEY

There are only two things that can happen with your money as you navigate your retirement years: You spend it, or you give it away. Although I talked about the "give it away" option first in the previous chapter, we like to encourage our clients to spend their money on themselves. Most don't have a spending plan.

This is so hard for the Midwestern Millionaires who are often the best savers but the worst spenders. Some of our clients—despite our assurances that their money will last as long as they do and our encouragement to spend more of it—are still not able to spend all their money. Even the clients who say "I want my last check to bounce, and I want to spend every dollar I have worked hard for" have a hard time spending all their money as it continues to grow over time.

Our clients want to enjoy their retirement, but they don't want to run out of money or be left without a legacy for their loved ones. For those clients, we put together formal spending plans so they can enjoy the money. We give them a budget that's more than they ever would have expected to spend.

This inability to spend has always fascinated me. I can't imagine it being hard to spend money. But then I see these Midwestern Millionaires—trained all their life to be frugal and save money—flip the switch in retirement and begin to spend. It's unbelievably difficult for them! A true paradigm shift. It's hard for them to watch their accounts go down when they've always seen them go up. And since they don't know how long they'll live, and don't know what the impacts of inflation or future healthcare costs will be for them, they hesitate to overspend today.

Peak Stamp of Approval

For many of our clients, spending plans aren't enough. We needed to create a "Peak Retirement Planning, Inc. APPROVED!" stamp for those who have trouble spending their hard-earned money (see picture). We send this as a fun gesture to clients to help encourage them to splurge on things like vacations, home renovations, toys such as a boat, or maybe something as small as buying blueberries when they are not on sale! One of our clients let us know that his wife now uses this stamp every time she wants to buy a new pair of shoes. Another client told us receiving this stamp made them laugh and smile at the same time. This is the type of fun relationship we love having with our clients. A relationship where they are living out their dreams, vision, mission . . . and purpose.

Dream, Vision, Mission . . . and Purpose

We help our clients realize their dreams, vision, and mission with what we call our "purpose of money" tool. Before we discuss this tool, I must explain the conversation we have with people when they first become clients and also every successive year of our relationship in serving them. We find out the true purpose for their money. This often includes a dream of traveling, a vision of spending time with grandkids, and a mission of staying healthy throughout retirement.

We then ask them how we can take the money they have to help enhance those desires. This involves putting together the spending plan so they can live out their goals. We hold them accountable each year to do what they tell us they want.

Remember, these people have been content in their level of spending all their lives. They've been content with their frugality. Now they need to be encouraged and challenged to do what they truly want. We will challenge them to "experiment" with what they talk about doing to see how it goes. After they have been frugal all their lives and shoveled money into their savings, we take pride in educating and teaching them the importance of shoveling the other way with their money so they can enjoy it. We expect them to show us pictures of the trips they take and see the opportunities they're providing for the grandkids. This holds them accountable but also allows us to see the value in the planning we're doing, which is extremely meaningful and why we do what we do.

There is no secret. One concern we always hear is "Do I have enough?" And most of the time we're telling the Midwestern Millionaire, "Yes, you have more than enough." We prove it to them by using a tool we've created called the "purpose of money calculator."

I'll walk you through this tool with a real family.

This couple, both sixty years old, have saved $3 million. They receive $70,000 per year total from both of their Social Security benefits, and they need $10,000 a month to live on.

THE PURPOSE OF MONEY

Twelve months times $10,000 per month means they need $120,000 per year. Since they have the guarantee of $70,000, we need to get them $50,000 more annual income from the $3 million they've saved up.

Based on a simple calculation known as the 4 percent rule, you know if you have $1,250,000 set aside, then you can generate $50,000 of income for the rest of your life.

$1,250,000 times 4 percent = $50,000

This calculation isn't perfect, but it at least gives you a good idea of how much cash you can spend without running out of money.

Let's move to the following chart, "Giving Your Money Purpose," where you will see three columns.

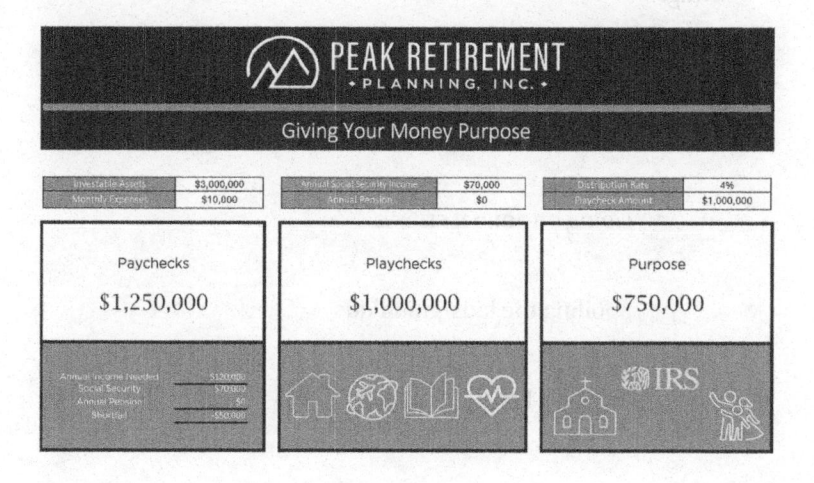

PEAK RETIREMENT
◆ PLANNING, INC. ◆

Giving Your Money Purpose

Investable Assets	$3,000,000	Annual Social Security Income	$70,000	Distribution Rate	4%
Monthly Expenses	$10,000	Annual Pension	$0	Paycheck Amount	$1,000,000

Paychecks	Playchecks	Purpose
$1,250,000	$1,000,000	$750,000

Annual Income Needed	$120,000
Social Security	$70,000
Annual Pension	$0
Shortfall	-$50,000

111

In the left column, the $1,250,000 falls under "paychecks"—also known as your retirement income plan. The chart shows the monthly expenses that need to be paid—all the bills, expenses, and necessities. The paycheck money is for needs.

The center column is your "playchecks," and no, that's not a typo. Playchecks consist of the money specifically set aside for those fun expenses—things and activities we don't need, but we want. We often encourage our Midwestern Millionaire clients to put more money in the playchecks column. They've worked hard for their money, and they should benefit from their labor and their conscientious saving. As you'll recall, these clients won't spend all their money when we run analyses like this.

The playcheck category could include a lot of different things:

- Traveling, including airfares, hotels, restaurants, and attractions

- Going on annual cruises

- Spoiling the kids/grandkids

- Buying a boat

- Buying a newer car

- Buying a second (vacation) home

- Investing in your health with a gym membership, a personal trainer, or a nutritionist

The playcheck is there for you to buy experiences and spend money on whatever makes your life easier and more joyful. We had a client spend $70,000 for a 121-day cruise around the world. I would say they're definitely maximizing their playchecks.

The playcheck category could also be considered an extra emergency fund for those items that are less fun, like surprise healthcare costs in the future or unexpected housing expenses like a new roof.

In this example on the chart, the clients told us if they had $1 million, they would be more than happy. I think it will be a big challenge for them to spend that playcheck fund, as that would mean an extra $40,000 (assuming the 4 percent rule) on top of the $50,000 for their paycheck amount they would have to spend. Including the $70,000 from their Social Security, they have a total of $160,000 to comfortably spend each year for everything they may need or want. Remember, they're frugal and diligent Midwestern Millionaires who struggle to spend that much money. If that's the case, we have sectioned off $2,250,000 for their lifetimes and have gotten an understanding that should be more than they need.

That brings us to the third column on the chart. What are we going to do with the rest of the $750,000? Well, that's where you can get creative. This is your "purpose" check. Some of our clients call it their "legacy fund" since whatever is left here would go to their kids or charities.

Note that the IRS logo is shown in the purpose section. It may not be your purpose to leave Uncle Sam more money than is needed, but unfortunately, those who don't plan may end up leaving more of this purpose check to the IRS than they intend to. The good news is that through proper tax planning, as discussed in this book, you can minimize Uncle Sam as beneficiary of your accounts and instead maximize the legacy to your loved ones as beneficiaries to ensure they get the most they can.

Now, with the purpose section, you need to think of this as your fund for not only giving when you pass but also potential gifting during your lifetime to loved ones or charities. Doing such giving or gifting could reduce your potential estate tax liability, as mentioned in an earlier chapter. Or maybe the money would be better used for your children's families now. It could allow your kids to have the funds to help pay for your grandchildren's college, or to start or grow their business, or buy a car without the extra expense of a car loan. You could give to your charities now and witness the impact your resources are making.

You can't take it with you.

You can only spend it or give it away.

I encourage you to think more about the purpose of the wealth you have accumulated. Challenge yourself about what is realistic and likely to happen over the years of your retirement, then find a retirement planning team that wants to see you live out your purpose, not just manage your investments.

One last thought on this idea: How would you feel if you were twenty years in the future, and you say to yourself, "I wish I had spent more money in retirement and done the things I wanted when I was healthy and able. But unfortunately, I never got around to it." Is that the retirement you want to live? You only get one try at it, and you won't be here forever.

One of our clients said to us as we were going through this exercise, "I probably said no to my kids too much when they were younger. If I could go back, I would say yes more, give them more, and allow them to have more opportunity." A sad realization, but she couldn't take it back.

The good news is because of your sacrifices and success as diligent savers over the years, you now have the opportunity to ensure that your retirement is full of purpose. I call this being financially free, and it should feel incredible. You won the accumulation game.

I have to say it: I asked myself whether I should put this chapter at the beginning of the book rather than near the end. But once our clients go through the steps with us, formalize their retirement plan, and see how much tax they can save and how much more they have to spend than they previously imagined—they finally see how much they can achieve with their hard-earned money. They feel more optimistic. They realize their "wish list" or their "bucket list" of activities and actions for their retirement years doesn't have to be wishful thinking but can be actual goals they can achieve—and pay for.

Imitate the Midwestern Millionaire: Get expert, holistic financial planning help. Reduce your tax burden across the board and for life. Enjoy yourself in retirement as you keep more of your hard-earned money—and then spend it or give the way you've dreamed you could.

11

WHY PEOPLE WORK WITH US (OR WITH A HOLISTIC TEAM LIKE US)

Our firm isn't like others in the financial industry. Most try to turn everyone they see into a client. We say we cannot help everyone. We're committed to serving those Midwestern Millionaires who we can benefit the most with our signature 5 Pillar Approach.

The most important pillar, as I've shown throughout this book, is tax planning. Taxes affect all your money and therefore affect every other pillar. Taxes affect your retirement income and your spending. Taxes affect your healthcare in retirement as well. Taxes must be planned for so you can create your desired legacy and organize your estate without any tax burden on your beneficiaries.

It is unfortunately true that not all advisors know how to perform such comprehensive tax efficiency for their clients. We know how to do that well, and it's obviously the biggest focus and foundation of our firm. That's one big reason people work with us.

As mentioned, our firm specializes in serving those who are diligent savers and have amassed more than the average person—the Midwestern Millionaire. We specifically work with those in or near retirement. We're more like the surgeon than the family doctor. That is, we're specialists who don't work with everyone, so we can focus and do our best work for those we do. Extreme laser-like focus.

As you've learned, Midwestern Millionaires require advanced, sophisticated planning. They need a team approach (several surgeons and specialists working in sync) and not just one individual trying to do everything for them (the family doctor). When I first started Peak Retirement Planning, Inc., it was just me. I quickly realized my clients would suffer if I didn't add great team members, advisors, and other professionals with complementary knowledge and expertise. There's only so much one individual can do. I couldn't run a business, serve clients, bring on new clients, prepare taxes, create legal documents, or be an expert on every part of a client's plan.

As our team has grown, we've been able to diversify our service offerings and give clients more services in one place. Our goal has always been to give the people we can best serve the best experience they can find. Having a team approach means we won't miss anything—multiple people are looking at each client's financial plan. Even one or two mistakes for the Midwestern Millionaire can be costly. That's why focused, diligent planning is needed for them, along with extreme attention to detail.

The other main reason people work with us is our shared values. People like to work with people who are like them. All things being equal, people work with someone they like and trust.

Those working with us also get to a point in their life where they say they would rather enjoy their retirement than plan their retirement. As we know, retirement planning can be complex. There are many decisions to make.

You want to be honest with yourself and ask if you're willing to do the work it takes to be the best steward of your life savings. Answer these questions:

1. Will you read and understand the tax code with its several thousand pages?

2. Will you stay up-to-date on all tax code changes as you must, since it's written in pencil?

3. Will you do the research and due diligence needed when it comes to choosing and changing your investments—and know where and how to do that?

4. Do you know what estate planning documents you need to protect your wealth and reduce taxes—and how to draft and file them properly so they are legally recognized as your wishes?

5. Do you know which accounts you will take income out of in retirement and the tax impact of it—so your money lasts as long as you do?

If you feel confident answering yes to these questions, great! You probably don't need help. If you already have a team you feel confident can you help with all those questions, then great as well. If you don't feel confident, you should probably seek help, whether that's a team like us or someone else who does this level of planning.

Another big reason successful people work with us is to ensure their spouse is financially taken care of if something were to happen to them—and to be informed on what those measures are. Oftentimes, we see one of the spouses is more hands-on with the retirement planning, and the other would be lost without their spouse. We offer peace of mind. We are the surviving spouse's go-to resource and trusted guide to handle all financial and tax issues upon their spouse's death.

When the hands-on spouse chooses us to help them, they know we can be trusted when they are no longer here. If this decision isn't made, the less-involved spouse would need to choose a firm that has the capabilities to serve their unique situation. They may not have enough understanding to make the best decision—especially considering how many people out there call themselves financial advisors but only manage investments or sell insurance products. They may not even be fiduciaries. I wouldn't call those people trusted guides. You need to be careful about who you trust in this industry. These are your life savings we're talking about. Every Midwestern Millionaire needs a financial planning team that is independent and comprehensive.

Being available to our clients is vital for us. People will leave a financial planner when there is a lack of communication. We are planning and managing our clients' life savings, which is obviously a big deal, so our clients have access to us for any and all questions and needs. We get back to our clients within twenty-four hours. We do a deep dive into their planning every year and always update them on their comprehensive 5 pillar plan. At that time, we also deliver a complete tax plan for the year.

Being proactive is also key to us. We have quarterly touchpoints with our clients where we proactively make adjustments and changes to their plans based on tax law changes or the client's own life changes, and we also discuss and potentially implement new planning strategies to their advantage.

People love our comprehensive and holistic approach, but more than anything, they like the collaboration with other professionals and our being a one-stop shop. They love the family office feel. We have two financial planners or professionals in every session who will offer different perspectives and ensure nothing is missed. Our advisors work together with our clients, and we look at our clients' financial plans together. We don't leave the work and responsibility to one person like other firms may do. We take a team approach.

We like to tell clients we do everything for them but cut their grass. (Hmm... maybe we'll offer that service sometime soon.)

I'll end with one last story from one of our clients. He had been with his financial planner for twenty years before coming to us. Naturally, I asked him why he decided to leave his close friend.

"First, you have shown me strategies and explained them so clearly to me," he said, "all the while leaving the choice of using them to me. My advisor has never even mentioned these strategies. Second, your team will be here for my retirement, my wife's retirement, and my kids' retirement. My advisor is older than me and about to retire soon."

I have a sense of humor, so I said, "We'll probably be here for your grandkids' retirements, too, so I hope you are fine with that as well."

I love sharing this story because it exemplifies one of our goals: to develop lifelong, generational relationships with our clients and to ensure their legacy can live on past their lifetimes.

Our clients often tell us they're tired of finding new dentists, doctors, lawyers, CPAs, and financial planners. They want to work with a team who will not only be there for them but also go the extra mile. That's why I started Peak Retirement Planning, Inc.

If you consider yourself a Midwestern Millionaire and feel the type of planning we do is what you're looking for, please schedule a time with our team at https://peakretirementplanning.com.

Congratulations on being a Midwestern Millionaire! Best of luck planning and protecting your hard-earned life savings.

A Sneak Preview of Joe's National Bestselling Book,

I HATE TAXES

INTRODUCTION

Anyone may arrange his affairs so that his taxes shall be as low as possible; he is not bound to choose that pattern which best pays the treasury. There is not even a patriotic duty to increase one's taxes.

Over and over again the Courts have said that there is nothing sinister in so arranging affairs as to keep taxes as low as possible. Everyone does it, rich and poor alike; and all do right, for nobody owes any public duty to pay more than the law demands.

Learned Hand (1872–1961), judge, US Court of Appeals[1]

You know the old saying "It's not what you know but who you know"? Well, in my business of retirement planning, our saying is "It's not how much you *make*, it's how much you *keep*."

---

1   Gregory v. Helvering 69 F.2d 809, 810 (2d Cir. 1934), aff'd, 293 U.S. 465, 55 S.Ct. 266, 79 L.Ed. 596 (1935)

That's what this book is all about. You've worked hard all your life, but I can tell you without even knowing you or your situation that you're probably giving away much more of your hard-earned money to Uncle Sam than you need to.

My job, my whole team's purpose, is to help you turn that around.

People are vastly different, but there's one thing we all have in common, no matter our background, age, race, gender, belief system, or profession:

**We all hate taxes.
And we all want to know how we can pay less.**

Don't get me wrong. I'll pay my fair share of taxes. I love this country, appreciate my citizenship, and will pay my taxes accordingly. I'm grateful for the opportunities I have in this country and the ease of life my family and I enjoy.

So let's be clear: We're not talking about "tax evasion," which means breaking the rules. We're talking about "tax avoidance," which means being smart about what the rules say. This is about knowing what tools the US Tax Code makes available to us, using them properly, and paying only our fair share. We would never encourage you to do things that would send you to jail.

As a US citizen, your tax avoidance is not only legal but necessary. It's your patriotic duty. The less you send to the government, the more you can spend and invest the way you choose and the more you can control. That could create jobs and wealth for our economy. I see saving money on taxes as a way to invest in America and make it a better place.

If I can legally understand what the tax code says and find loopholes to save money, then what do you think I'm going to do? I work hard for my money, and so do you. This is your life savings we're talking about. We need to be as diligent as possible to keep more money in your pocket and less in Uncle Sam's. Because guess what? He's not your real uncle.

Now, if you enjoy paying taxes and want to pay more, I'm afraid this book isn't for you. You would be better off staying status quo and sending in a donation to the IRS every year above what you pay in taxes. I'm also more than happy to give you a refund for this book.

This book—and all the planning my firm does for our clients—is about how to limit Uncle Sam's take from your pocket in retirement.

My Three Goals for This Book

1. Motivate you to be proactive with your tax planning so that you have your own plan and not the IRS's plan.
2. Get you to the 0 percent tax bracket. This is what I call getting legally divorced from the IRS for life.
3. Save you potentially $100,000+ in tax planning.

I HATE TAXES

Don't tip Uncle Sam. Pay your fair share but not a penny more—keep your hard-earned life savings in your pocket.

CHAPTER 1
WHY ACT NOW?

> *Collecting more taxes than is absolutely necessary is legalized robbery.*
>
> **Calvin Coolidge, thirtieth president of the United States, 1923–1929**

To express the duty that you must pay the least amount of taxes—only the amount you owe—I went to the IRS website. The Taxpayer Bill of Rights literally includes, "The Right to Pay No More than the Correct Amount of Tax."[2]

The right! I will exercise that right to pay no more than the correct amount of tax.

The *I Hate Taxes* book title comes from one of our clients—I'll call her Jeannie—after she chose to trust us with her life savings. It was one of those memorable moments you never forget. Jeannie stopped me cold near the start of our

---

2   https://www.irs.gov/taxpayer-bill-of-rights.

session and looked me dead in the eye. Her voice raised, she said to me, "Joe, there's one thing I want you to know about me. I hate taxes. I don't like anything about them. I don't like how they're spent, and I don't want to pay for things I disagree with. I want to pay the least amount possible. I want to spend my money on what matches my values and beliefs, and I don't trust the government."

She's right.

The other problem with taxes is that sometimes they don't make sense. For example, tax benefits are given to people who make a positive impact on the environment, such as buying an electric car. Yet people are also given a tax benefit for buying a gas-guzzling RV motorhome, which has the opposite impact. A popular tax benefit is charitable gifting, which I heartily agree with and love what it can do for our country, but other benefits are less clear. Who's making these rules? Which rules are best? What are we truly incentivizing? Do the incentives match your values? Not always the case for me.

CHAPTER 2

WE'RE DIFFERENT FROM OTHER PLANNERS

I've made it my mission—and the mission of our firm at Peak Retirement Planning, Inc.—to help people pay the least amount of taxes over their lifetime. Our mission differentiates us from the masses, as many financial planners and CPAs won't talk about tax planning at all.

> Tax planning isn't talked about enough.

Why aren't taxes talked about? For many, they'll be their biggest expense over their lifetime. Why then won't financial planners and CPAs bring these strategies to the table for you? We'll discuss why this is the case in chapter 20, so stay tuned.

Everyone's situation is unique. Married or single. Dependents or not. Deductibles or none. Different incomes make what I'm about to cite challengeable, but here goes:

Among the more than 164 million Americans who filed tax returns in 2020, the average federal income tax payment was $16,615, according to the most recent Internal Revenue Service data.[3]

Do the math over forty years of your active working life. That's $664,600. And that's an average of all tax-paying Americans. Ask yourself, did I even pay that much for my home? Not likely.

And still, many of you are scoffing, thinking that you've paid far more than that—and you would be right.

> **Here's the real question to ask:
> Did we need to pay that much?**

And here's the other question to ask: Are we truly paying our fair share?

If you review the following chart from the Tax Foundation website, it may show that you're paying well more than what others are paying. Fifty percent of taxpayers pay on average a 3.1 percent tax rate. I would imagine you're paying much more than that considering you're reading a book about hating taxes and saving money.

---

[3] "How much income tax does the average American pay the IRS?" Liz Knueven, Business Insider, Updated February 1, 2023, https://www.businessinsider.com/personal-finance/average-federal-income-tax-payment-by-income.

High-Income Taxpayers Paid the Highest Average Income Tax Rates

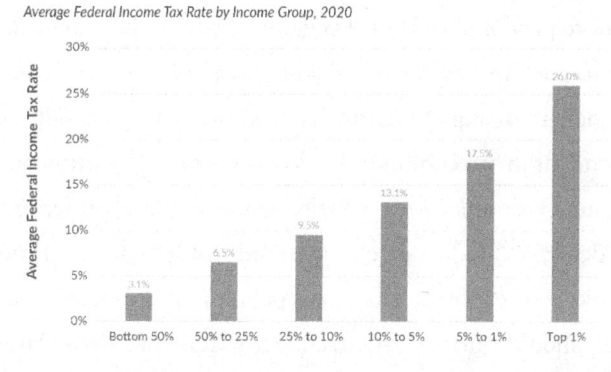

Average Federal Income Tax Rate by Income Group, 2020

Income Group	Average Federal Income Tax Rate
Bottom 50%	3.1%
50% to 25%	6.5%
25% to 10%	9.5%
10% to 5%	13.1%
5% to 1%	17.5%
Top 1%	26.0%

TAX FOUNDATION @TaxFoundation

Source: "Summary of the Latest Federal Income Tax Data," Erica York, January 26, 2023, https://taxfoundation.org/publications/latest-federal-income-tax-data/.

I agree with the biblical reference of Luke 12:48, "To whom much is given, much will be required," and so I'll pay my fair share. But is it fair to penalize people who work hard and save money and reward people who don't work hard or save money? I would rather save money on taxes that aren't always used for my personal convictions and instead use that tax savings toward what I feel can make a true impact in this world.

If you hate taxes, don't avoid the IRS; instead, play their own game at an expert level.

At Peak Retirement Planning, Inc., our experts know how to play (and win) the tax game. We know how to make an impact and help hardworking people keep their hard-earned life savings. Our firm delivers hundreds of workshops each year in our communities. We're constantly putting out content via our *Joe Knows Retirement* YouTube channel and podcast, TV, radio, articles featured in Kiplinger, and the books I write. I've seen too many people pay more taxes than they should, and we want to change that before it's too late.

During my years in financial planning, I've come to realize that there are two types of people who don't pay taxes: poor people and smart people. If you're poor, you reach a point where your income is so low that the government doesn't ask you for income taxes. If you're smart, you could live a tax-free retirement by understanding the rules and giving yourself enough time to plan. Being smart doesn't involve being poor.

We have a widowed client right now, Sarah, who has $1 million in her retirement accounts and will pay no more taxes for the rest of her life. This is what she and I call "legally divorcing the IRS for the rest of your life."

We can help many of our clients get to this spot. Sarah certainly isn't poor, but extremely smart financially. She has followed our advice over the years to get to where she needs to be. You may have heard that the rich also don't pay taxes. This annoys some, but I applaud them for being smart. The rich don't pay taxes because they hire smart people to show them strategies to reduce their taxes. Maybe you should do that yourself.

It's not what you know but who you know, right? Not only that: It isn't how much you make, it's how much you keep.

> **In short, when it comes to the rich, don't hate the player, hate the game.**

There are loopholes in the US Tax Code for everyone—if you're smart enough to find them.

And, if like Sarah you have over $1 million net worth, then you're in the top 10 percent of our country's wealth.[4] Hate it or love it, you're wealthy. And most of your wealth is in tax-deferred investments with your partner Uncle Sam.

You better get busy planning. Hundreds of thousands of your dollars are on the line. If you're a saver and have done the right thing, then you're being desensitized. The tax system has penalized savers and benefited non-savers. That's criminal, if you ask me. The IRS can change the rules on us at any time.

Change Is Hard

Sometimes we know we need to change, and we don't want to. For some, you might know you need to eat healthily, but

---

[4] "33 Incredible Millionaire Statistics [2023]: 8.8% of US Adults Are Millionaires," Abby McCain, February 24, 2023, https://www.zippia.com/advice/millionaire-statistics/.

you would rather go for the dessert, or you might know you need to get off your phone or social media, but you can't because you're addicted.

When it comes to taxes (and other things), inaction is the worst kind of action. The biggest advice I can give you through this book is to *get help*. The US Tax Code is complex. There are more words in the tax code than the Bible. Do you know what all the words mean? Have you ever even read it? If not, you're at risk of losing money and susceptible to government control, with less money in your pocket long term.

I cover tax-planning strategies in this book and will try to make them seem easy, but understand there is much more to it, and I'm only providing general information. Everyone's situation is specific, and everything I say in this book will be different for different people.

In my life, I try to delegate everything I'm not an expert at. I go to a doctor to perform surgery on me, I go to a mechanic to change my oil, and I have a team clean my house. I'm not good at cleaning, and I don't want to spend five hours on a Saturday doing it. I would rather spend my Saturdays writing tax books.

My point is, are you really going to have the time to understand how to make the smartest decisions financially with a full-time job, family responsibilities, hobbies, and other obligations? From what I see, that's a recipe for disaster. If you're not on top of tax planning, you could miss saving hundreds of thousands of dollars over your lifetime. My goal with this book is to create a paradigm shift. Everyone is telling you not to pay taxes, but I'm going to tell you to pay your taxes now so you don't have to pay them later.

The IRS's Plan or Your Plan?

You have a decision to make. You can follow the status quo and ignore the opportunities at your fingertips—what we would consider the IRS's plan. The IRS's plan could cost you lots of money in mistakes over time as discussed earlier. Or you can follow your own plan where you know what's being done and when it's being done. Your plan could save you money on taxes. At the end of the day, your actions will decide your financial future.

After reading this book, talk with us at Peak Retirement Planning, Inc. The book is meant to open your eyes and prod you into action as you learn about basic and advanced strategies that may be a good fit for your circumstances. We're here for you.

PEAK RETIREMENT
◆ PLANNING, INC. ◆

RESOURCES FROM
PEAK RETIREMENT PLANNING, INC.

READ

Read our Amazon bestselling books, "I Hate Taxes" and "Midwestern Millionaire".

Browse our articles that are featured in National Kiplinger publications for financial tips and more!

KIPLINGER

WATCH

Watch us weekly on the news where we discuss important retirement strategies.

Find us on YouTube, where we publish educational videos for those in or near retirement every week!

YOUTUBE

LISTEN

Listen online or on the radio to hear us discuss your top retirement concerns.

NEWS RADIO 610 WTVN

Tune in to our educational podcast "Joe Knows Retirement."

PODCAST

---

www.peakretirementplanning.com | info@peakretirementplanning.com

We are an independent financial services firm helping individuals create retirement strategies using a variety of investment and insurance products to custom-suit their needs and objectives. Investment Advisory Services and Insurance Services are offered through Peak Retirement Planning, Inc., a Registered Investment Advisor.

ABOUT THE AUTHOR

Joe F. Schmitz Jr., CFP®, ChFC®, CKA® is the founder and CEO of Peak Retirement Planning, Inc., in Columbus, Ohio.

Joe has built a comprehensive retirement planning company focused on helping clients grow and preserve their wealth. Under Joe's leadership, a team of experienced financial professionals use tax-efficient strategies, investment management, income planning, proactive healthcare planning, and estate planning to help clients feel confident in their financial future and the legacy they leave behind.

As a CERTIFIED FINANCIAL PLANNER®, Joe has passed a rigorous education program and certification exam to receive the CFP® designation, and he also has well over the six thousand hours of professional experience required by the CFP® Board. What's more, Joe has received the designation of Certified Kingdom Advisor®, demonstrating that he has learned the finer points of retirement planning, investing, insurance, and taxation in accordance with Christian principles. He has created a firm that helps his clients have a deep sense of purpose in how they steward their wealth.

Joe got his start in the financial services industry in 2015. He graduated with a bachelor of science in finance and financial planning from Mount Vernon Nazarene University, where he played basketball and ran track. He has lived near Columbus his entire life.

When Joe isn't in the office, he can be found running, hiking, biking, or reading. He also enjoys traveling and spending time with family and friends. In addition, Joe sponsors and coaches a youth basketball team for Nova Village Athletic Club.

Made in the USA
Monee, IL
11 July 2025